The Soul Care Workbook is a powerful tool to help you and others work through and integrate into your life the deeper principles in *Soul Care – 7 Transformational Principles for a Healthy Soul.* Dr. Rob Reimer provides a practical guide that is sure to challenge and encourage you with biblical patterns and principles towards freedom and growth in Christ—for the partisan, pupil, small group leader, preacher, or proclaimer of faith in Christ.

—**Rev. Ken Graham** - *President, Christian and Missionary Alliance of Australia, Regional Coordinator, Asia Pacific Alliance Churches, Alliance World Fellowship*

I am a big believer in *Soul Care.* The reasons are numerous . . . the content is biblical; the Holy Spirit's anointing is upon Rob as he delivers the content; the fruit of life change is clearly evident. I regularly encourage everyone at Discovery Church to go through Soul Care. Rob has been with us on three separate occasions to host a Soul Care Conference. In addition, we hold classes two to three times a year using the conference via videotapes. The result: profound life-change for hundreds of people. As with most things in life, application is key. While great content is helpful, it's great application of great content that makes for profound life-change. In keeping with this desire and need for application, Rob has pulled together a Soul Care workbook. It's a resource aimed at application. Assuming you're in favor of application, I highly recommend it to you.

—**Don Cousins** - *Sr. Lead Pastor, Discovery Church, Orlando, Florida*

Since the Soul Care journey is made up of both healing and intentional pursuit of God, it isn't a microwaved faith. I love when Rob says, "You can have as much of Jesus you want, but it'll cost something." I'm so glad and grateful Rob turned his transformative teachings into a workbook that someone can lean into with practical applications either alone in a prayer room or in a discipleship group. As believers we all want more of God, but many people just don't know where to start their freedom and empowerment journey. This is another key tool for every local church and every believer. God will use it!

—**Dr. Tim Meier** - *The Christian and Missionary Alliance*

Ephesians 4:12 calls us to "equip the saints for the work of the ministry." My old mentor, John Wimber, used to say this means "the day of the superstar is over" and "everybody gets to play!" My buddy Rob gets this. His goal in life and this workbook is to train and empower a generation of Christ followers to advance the Kingdom of God and do damage to Satan's strongholds. Thank you, Rob. It's a good day in the Kingdom!

—**Ron Walborn, D.Min** - *Executive Director of Urban Initiatives for Asbury Seminary (NY), Asbury Theological Seminary*

THE SOUL CARE WORKBOOK

Dr. Rob Reimer

Carpenter's Son Publishing

The Soul Care Workbook

Published by Carpenter's Son Publishing, Franklin, Tennessee
ClovercroftPublishingGroup.com

Cover Design by Danielle Reimer Benninger

Edited by Robert Irvin

Interior Design by Suzanne Lawing

Printed in the United States of America

ISBN: 978-1-968127-02-2 (print)

CONTENTS

USING THIS SOUL CARE WORKBOOK

Over the years, many people have asked me to write a workbook that could be used alongside my book *Soul Care: 7 Transformational Principles for a Healthy Soul.* Some wanted me to write a volume that could be used to help them integrate these principles on a personal level; it would take them deeper into freedom in Christ. Others wanted me to develop a small group companion guide that would help small groups navigate through the book and/or the video teachings of Soul Care so they could take the principles deeper, together, as a group.

This book will serve both needs, and I will give some thoughts on how to use it alongside the book, the videos, and/or the Soul Care eCourse. You can use it by yourself to integrate the principles in your life, or you can use it with a group.

I often say that *Soul Care* is not a book to be read like a novel, nor a conference to be attended in three days. It is a lifestyle to be adopted and principles to be integrated into your daily existence. You are going to continue to sin, and you will need to keep walking in the light with God and others and practice repentance if you want to live free and have a healthy soul. You are going to continue to get hurt by others, and you are going to have to continue to bless those who curse you and forgive those who sin against you if you want to experience wholeness in life.

I did a lot of work on my identity in Christ, and overcoming the lies that I believed, when Jen and I went through a marriage crisis early in our ministry. I knew I was loved by God, but I had to learn how to live as a deeply loved person. This work changed our interactions and saved our marriage. But that is not the only time in my life I have had to work on my identity. I went through a season of attacks in ministry that lasted a number of years. All the attacks had the effect of chipping away at the foundation of my worth, and I had to repair the foundation by doing identity work. I had to do more identity work when COVID hit and all the Soul Care (and other) conferences were canceled. I was sitting on my porch day by day with no emails, no phone calls, no invites, and I realized that one day this would be the reality of my life, and no

Here is the point: the work of the soul is never done. It takes one day longer than a lifetime to finally become like Jesus.

one would invite me to come and do ministry anymore. But I knew these emotions connected to my identity, and I knew how to do the work of renewing my mind, so I was able to navigate through those times fairly quickly and come out the other side stronger and healthier. Here is the point: the work of the soul is never done. It takes one day longer than a lifetime to finally become like Jesus. When we meet Him face to face, we shall be like Him, but in the meantime, we are on a journey, and we have work to do. We have to keep integrating these principles into our lives. This workbook will help individuals and groups do just that.

If I was pastoring a church today, or leading a small group through Soul Care, this is how I would approach it (and this is certainly not the only way to do it): I would have people read the book, watch the corresponding videos together in their group, and then work through the workbook exercises to help them live out this material.[1] Repetition is integral to integration. I would probably take at least two weeks to cover each topic; you can do it all in one week, but it will certainly take you longer than a week or two to live out these principles. I know some small groups and/or churches that have spent at least one month on each topic before moving on because they really wanted to help their people apply these truths. I also know that I would keep coming back to these truths over and over again. I would not treat this as a program, run through it, and move on to the next program, but I would want to do my best as a leader to ensure I and all my parishioners are deeply integrating these principles.

There is also an eCourse for *Soul Care* (and *The Soul Care Leader*), and I know some of you will be using this workbook along with the Soul Care eCourse. My approach would be the same: read the book *Soul Care,* watch the video/videos on the same topic (e.g., identity), and work through the workbook. Keep doing the work until you are living the victorious life Jesus has purchased for you on the cross. Knowledge will not lead you to victory; you have to do the work. The exercises here and in the book, or in the eCourse, are all designed to help you do the work and live it out.

In this workbook I will open each chapter with the corresponding section in the book that you need to read, or the Soul Care Video Series that you need to watch, or the Soul Care eCourse videos that go along with the chapter. I will also include a summary of the topic at hand, which is not intended as a substitute for reading the chapter and/or watching the videos. It is simply a quick summary of what you have learned; it will include some new insights. So take the time to read and/or watch, then do the workbook. Finally, I will include some reflection questions and exercises that can help you incorporate these principles in your life. There will be space for journaling, reflecting, jotting notes, and prayers that can help you process these principles. This is truly a workbook; you

1 Note that there is one talk in the video series that is not in the book—that is a talk on intimacy with God. In the book I mention that I cover this topic of intimacy in other places, so to keep *Soul Care* a reasonable length, I excluded a chapter on it there. I will write a chapter here on intimacy, which will include exercises, and you can use the video and this chapter in your group.

have to do the work. Life change doesn't occur because you know these things; you have to live these things out to be transformed. It is designed to be used as a companion volume with the video teaching and/or the *Soul Care* book, and/or the Soul Care eCourse, to better help you apply these principles and become more free and full in Christ. It is not a standalone text.

In the Western church our approach to discipleship has been too cognitive. We are a knowledge-based discipleship culture, but Jesus was an obedience-based discipleship teacher. He was always pointing people to a lifestyle of following obediently after God. We have all too often substituted right knowledge for righteous living and learned behaviors for true transformation. We have too often asked the wrong questions. We have asked, "Do you know you are loved by God?" If you've ever been to church or read your Bible, you know the answer is yes. But it is the wrong question because it is merely a knowledge-based question and it assumes that if we believe the right things, we will do the right things. The real question that we need to ask is: *Are you living like a deeply loved person in all your human interactions?* In the Bible, true knowledge always leads to life change—we know it when we live it. Without obedience there isn't transformation. If we aren't living a principle out, then we are still learning about it. This workbook is geared to help you and the people you are doing life with live out these essential truths of Scripture that lead to freedom and fullness. James tells us that faith without deeds is dead. If we know we are loved by God but don't live like deeply loved people, then how has our faith benefited us? We must live it—this alone will produce deep life change.

But it is the wrong question because it is merely a knowledge-based question and it assumes that if we believe the right things, we will do the right things. The real question that we need to ask is: Are you living like a deeply loved person in all your human interactions?

God has called me to preach, lead, mentor, and write for the purpose of revival. That is my passion in life. All the tools that I seek to create are to lead to that end. This is no exception. I have discovered that by living out these principles I have more fulfillment, freedom, joy, fullness, and wholeness. Soul Care, by God's act, has become a life-change movement that has impacted hundreds of thousands of people around the world. I never set out to create a movement of life change. I never even set out to write books or do conferences. In the beginning, I was simply trying to save my marriage by becoming a healthier person and a better follower of Jesus, and God led me to discover these principles. For the most part, they were all things I knew; they were things I had read about in my Bible or heard growing up in church. I had been reading my Bible cover to cover every year since I was 16. I had been to seminary for my master's and doctoral degrees. I had been a pastor for several years. My problem wasn't that I didn't know these things; my problem was that I wasn't living these things out in a way that produced heart and soul change and led me to become the kind of person Jesus wanted me to be and my wife needed me to be. Living them has made all the difference. I have never been more content in life, ministry, or marriage.

That is why I wrote this volume. I deeply desire to help you to live out these principles that can produce transformation. God will do His part, but you have to do your part. Don't just read about these things or learn about these principles. Don't mail it in or assume you are living it because you know it.

Do the work. Do the hard work of the soul. Learn to live like a deeply loved person, chosen by God, in all of your human interactions and in all of life's circumstances. Learn to apply these principles in everyday life so you can live free and full in Christ. And may God bless you as you do the work.

One

INTIMACY WITH GOD

Preparation work for this chapter:

In the *Soul Care* book, there is no corresponding chapter to read. (You may, however, want to read chapter 1 in *The Soul Care Leader* for more on intimacy with God.)

In the Video series, watch the first video on intimacy with God

In the Soul Care eCourse, watch Lesson 4

As I look back on my journey toward freedom and fullness in Christ, it is clear to me that God's presence and power were critical elements in my formation. Only God can change the heart. So we must learn to access God's presence, his power, and his voice if we are going to experience deep life change. Depth with God is a choice we need to make and a price we need to pay.

In my book *Soul Care,* I do not have a chapter on intimacy with God. I mention the importance of God's presence and power for our life-change journey, but I refer people to other books I've written to go deeper into the subject of drawing near to God. But in the Soul Care eCourse I have some teaching on intimacy, as does the video series on Soul Care (accessible through Vimeo on Demand on our website, or the DVD). And at every Soul Care Conference I begin by talking about intimacy with God. I felt it was important to include a chapter on intimacy in this workbook.

In 2 Corinthians 3, Paul refers to an Old Testament story about Moses. You likely remember the story where Moses would go into the holy tabernacle, and there he would enter into the manifest presence of God and receive the word of the Lord for the people. When Moses came out of the Tabernacle, he was aglow! His face was shining with the presence of God. But the glory of God, the manifest presence of God, and the glowing effect it had would begin to fade from his face as he stepped out of God's presence. So Moses would come out of the tabernacle, speak the word of the Lord with his face shining with God's glory, and then put a veil over his face so the people couldn't see the glory fade. Paul writes to the church in Corinth, "We are not like Moses, who would put a veil over his face to prevent the Israelites from seeing the end of what was passing away" (2 Corinthians 3:13). We are not like Moses because we don't have to go in and out of the tabernacle to meet with God. We are the tabernacle. We carry the presence of God within us now because we are united with Christ, and his Holy Spirit has been deposited within us.

Paul goes on to say: "Now the Lord is the Spirit, and where the Spirit of the Lord is, there is freedom. And we all, who with unveiled faces contemplate the Lord's glory, are being transformed into his image with ever increasing glory, which comes from the Lord, who is the Spirit" (2 Corinthians 3:17, 18). Paul tells us that we are transformed by God's presence. We need to contemplate God's glory, God's presence, within us. We need to draw near to God because God's Spirit is life-changing. There is transformation in the manifest presence of God.

So how do we draw near to God? How do we experience his life-giving, transforming presence? I am going to share some key principles. It will have overlap with the eCourse, the video series, and the Soul Care Conferences, but I will cover some different things as well. The most important part of this workbook, and this chapter, is to drill down on application. So we will focus on that particularly.

A Healthy Spiritual Rhythm

If we are going to connect deeply with God and be transformed by abiding in his presence, we need to develop a healthy spiritual rhythm. Again, one of the problems in the church is that we too often ask the wrong questions. We ask people, "Are you spending time with God?" It is a good beginning question, but we have to go beyond that. Listen: the Pharisees spent time with God, and they killed Jesus! The question assumes that if we are spending time with God, we will become like Jesus. But that isn't always true. Here is a much better question: "Is your spiritual rhythm working?" Your spiritual rhythm is what you do on a daily, weekly, monthly, and yearly basis to connect deeply with God. What spiritual practices are you engaging in on a regular basis to draw near to God? How do you know if your rhythm is working? We will come back to this question shortly.

I have noticed that people who go deep with God have four things in common. They spend time alone with God in solitude. I can't get close to my wife without spending time with her, and it is the same in my relationship with God. So we need to engage in spiritual disciplines and spend time alone with God to get close to Him. Second, people who go deep with God spend time in silence with the Lord. It is a focused silence, an abiding in his presence, and listening for God to speak through the Word and the Spirit. Third, people who develop depth suffer wisely. You do not get to choose if you will suffer in life; you only get to choose how you suffer. Finally, people of depth sacrifice for God out of a heart full of love.

Time Alone with God

We have to develop a spiritual rhythm by engaging in certain spiritual practices, the goal of which is to cultivate intimacy with God. The disciplines we engage in are not an end in themselves; they are not a measure of maturity. They are merely a means to an end and an aide to maturity. These spiritual practices include things like worship and thanksgiving, Scripture reading, study and meditation, communion, attending church, living in community with other believers, silence, solitude, fasting, and spiritual retreats. That is not an all-inclusive list; these are just a sampling of spiritual practices we engage in so we can draw near to God.

Allow me to give just a couple of helpful pointers about constructing a healthy spiritual rhythm. **First, make sure you have the right goal when it comes to spiritual practices.** Your goal should be to enter God's presence, to connect with God in intimacy. The phrase I use for this goal is that I am seeking to "attend to God's presence" in every spiritual discipline I use. When I fast, the purpose isn't weight loss, or self-denial—those things can be a benefit—but my true goal is to attend to God's presence through that self-denial. When I read my Bible, the purpose of doing so isn't to know the Bible or to know about God; the purpose of reading my Bible is to encounter the living God. The Bible is not an end in itself; it is a means to an end. It is like a finger pointing to a sunset. We don't care to focus on the finger, we want to see the glory of the sunset. When we get to Heaven, we will no longer need our Bible because we will be with God Himself. That is our ultimate goal: being with God. So make sure when you go to spend time with God that you have this goal set deep in your heart and mind.

The Bible is not an end in itself; it is a means to an end. It is like a finger pointing to a sunset.

Second, we must pursue God's face, not merely God's hands. There have been too many times in my life where my relationship with God was too focused on asking God for things. "God, give me this" or "God, give me that." "God, fix this problem" or "Give me wisdom." "God, heal this person, save that person, help me here, help me there." There is nothing wrong with asking God for things; He is a good Father and He has told us to come to Him with our requests. In the Lord's prayer Jesus told us to ask for our daily bread, but He also began the entire prayer relationally: "Our Father, who is in heaven." There came a point in my spiritual journey where I realized I needed to spend more time seeking God's face if I was going to draw near to God. This is how the kingdom of God works: when Jesus shows up, the kingdom comes. When we show up, nothing happens. Jesus said that apart from Him we can do nothing (John 15). So if I want to see more kingdom activity in my life, the key is that I abide with Jesus so closely that I become marked by his presence so that, when I show up, Jesus shows up and the kingdom comes.

I discovered the key to abiding was seeking God's face, not merely his hands. I had to spend more time seeking to draw near to Jesus. This meant I needed to change some of the spiritual practices I was engaging in.

I have found a few practices to be particularly helpful in seeking God's face: (1) *worship and thanksgiving.* Often, I do not sing songs, I simply let worship music play and just try to soak in God's presence. I fix my attention on Jesus, enter God's presence, and linger with Him. (2) *Scripture praying and meditation.* I shifted from simply reading and studying Scripture (I still do these two things) to praying and meditating on Scripture. I wait for the illumination of the Spirit, and I linger there in God's presence. Paul said that "All Scripture is God-breathed" (2 Timothy 3:16). I am waiting for the breath of God to blow fresh revelation in my spirit. A word, phrase, or idea jumps out at me from the Bible; I sense an inner stirring of the Spirit, and I linger with that passage until God speaks to me through the Word and the Spirit about what He is trying to reveal to me. I began praying Scripture by praying the Psalms, since they are a prayer book, and I found that helpful to seeking God's face. (3) *Silence*: I have discovered that sitting alone with God in silence, just fixing my loving attention on Jesus, has been helpful to draw near to Him. I don't ask for anything, nor am I necessarily even trying to listen to God speak. I am just lingering slowly in his presence. (4) *Listening prayer.* It is hard to have intimacy with anyone if the conversation is a monologue. Intimacy requires a dialogue. So I want to hear God through the Scriptures, and I want to hear God directly through the Spirit. I am giving God space to communicate to me directly so I can draw near to Him. For many years I have spent at least a few minutes alone with God each day cultivating an awareness of God's presence and pausing to listen for his voice.

Third, we must persist in our pursuit of God. I meet with God every day, and I have done it for four decades. Jesus said, "If you, then, though you are evil, know how to give good gifts to your children, how much more will your Father in heaven give the Holy Spirit to those who ask him!" (Luke 11:13). You can have as much of God as you want, but no more than you're willing to pay the price for. There is always more of God; God is infinite and eternal, so you can always learn more about God, experience more of God, encounter God afresh and anew. Heaven will not be boring because God is infinite. Ten thousand years from now in Heaven we will discover something about God's love that we had never seen before. We will have been there with God for ten thousand years and we will discover something completely new about his love! And one million years later we will make a brand new discovery about some aspect of the love of God. Here we will have been with God for a million years, and we will still be discovering new things about his unfathomable love. Why? Because God is infinite and eternal; you can't tap God. One of the implications of this is that if my relationship

You can have as much of God as you want, but no more than you're willing to pay the price for. There is always more of God.

with God gets boring, it isn't because God is boring! That's on me. But another implication is that we must persist in our pursuit of God, because there is always more. We cannot become complacent if we want to go deep in intimacy. We have to find ways to ignite our passion to pursue God.

If you pursue God for deeper levels of intimacy, you will run into times when you feel stuck. Inevitably, you will feel plateaued and find your time with God becomes dry, and you feel like you're wandering through the desert. Do not quit. You must persist in pursuit. You will run into spiritual seasons of disappointment and hurt, and you will have to sort out grief and get through your disappointment, heartache, and offense with God. The temptation will be to harden your heart and take a step back. But do not quit. Press in and press through. There will be times when you feel complacent and apathetic, and you will want to coast and settle for "good enough." Again: *don't quit.* Reignite your spiritual fire and come after God with all your heart. He is worth it. You must persist in your pursuit.

Fourth, in developing a healthy rhythm I have found it is essential to go through an empty/fill cycle. I like to use the metaphor that your soul is like a suitcase. Too often we are coming to God asking for more, but the suitcase of our soul is already filled. We haven't emptied it. We are seeking God for more of Himself, more peace, more joy, more love, more freedom and fullness. But God can't give us more because our suitcase is already full—full of hurt, lies, fears, and other things that hinder us from God's fullness. We need to empty the suitcase first. In Ephesians 4 Paul told us to put off our old self before we put on our new self in Christ. Paul spent the first three chapters of Ephesians talking about our new identity in Christ, but we do not become this new person automatically; we have to do the work. We have to empty before we can fill.

Every day I do three things in my time with God to help empty the suitcase of my soul. (1) *I pray through my to-do list.* If I don't, the things I have to do will distract me from giving Jesus my full and undivided attention. Praying through my to-do list allows me to empty it from my heart so it won't distract me, and it also makes me more sensitive to the Spirit's direction when I am doing those things later in the day. (2) *I make sure my confessions are current.* I ask God to show me if there is any sin, and I bring it to Jesus. Jesus made this part of his model prayer: "Forgive us our debts, as we also have forgiven our debtors" (Matthew 6:12). Sin quenches the Spirit's flow in my life, and it hinders me from intimacy. (3) *I pray through my negative emotions.* Every day I process my negative emotions with God. I have discovered often that the earliest indicator that something is "off" in my soul is a negative emotion. When I am walking in step with the Spirit, I experience the fruit of the Spirit, and these begin with love, joy, and peace. But when I am out of alignment with the Spirit, I no longer experience love, joy, and peace, but instead irritation, aggravation, annoyance, anxiety, fear, and more negative emotions. This is why I process my negative emotions every day; they often indicate where I am getting out of alignment with God. I ask God to show me why I feel what I feel, and I process through until I get to the root issue and then resolve that with God. In and of themselves, the emotions are not bad. They are just emotions, but they are often indicative of some root issues that need to be processed or they will interfere with my intimacy with Jesus.

Let me go back to the key question: is your rhythm working? How do you know if it is working? (1) *Begin with love.* Jesus said the most important thing is to love God and love people (Matthew 22:37-39). So, if you are drawing near to God, you should become a more loving person. Is Jesus your first love and primary obsession? Do you love God and love people more than you did two years ago? If not, then there is something off in your soul, and you may still be doing all sorts of spiritual things, but they are not producing the results they should. (2) *Are you experiencing freedom and fullness in Christ?* Jesus said that He came to set the captives free, and He came to give us life and life abundant. So when I am abiding in Jesus, I should experience freedom and fullness. Are you more free and full than you were a year ago? (3) *Are you sensing God's presence and hearing God's voice?* Jesus deposited his Spirit in us and told us that his sheep would hear his voice (John 10:27). He told us the Holy Spirit would speak to us, lead us, guide us, convict us, and communicate to us in a variety of ways (John chapters 14-16). So if I am in step with the Spirit and drawing near, I should be experiencing God's presence and hearing God's voice. Is that true in your life? (4) *Are you experiencing love, joy, and peace?* These are the emotions of the Spirit. When I am walking in the Spirit, I experience love, joy, and peace. When I get out of alignment with the Spirit, I experience irritation, aggravation, annoyance, anger, anxiety, fear, and the like. That is not the fruit of the Spirit. This is why I process my negative emotions every day—to make sure I keep my heart in alignment with God so I can consistently experience love, joy, and peace. As I said earlier, those negative emotions are often the earliest indicator that something is off in my soul. They are a gift to me—if I process them well and figure out what is underneath.

Is Jesus your first love and primary obsession? Do you love God and love people more than you did two years ago?

If your rhythm isn't working, what do you do? Here are two important keys to help.

(1) *Change it.* This isn't rocket science, but religious people so often just keep doing the same spiritual rhythm day in and day out while they are stuck, stagnant, and stale. It's as if they are hoping that if they just keep doing the same routine, something will change. As I already said, please hear me: you have to persist in pursuit. So the right answer is not to quit; the right answer is to adjust your rhythm. Perhaps you are spiritually plateaued because your rhythm is old, tired, and worn out. When you get stuck, go to God and ask Him what to change. I simply pray, "Lord, my rhythm isn't working. I feel stuck. What should I change?" Then I wait for insight from the Lord, and I do whatever He tells me to do. My most recent change was a sense that I needed to go back to praying the Psalms. I will do that for a while in my time with God, but like all routines, it can become stale, so I have to change it up. I had stopped doing it previously because it felt stale to me, but I sensed it

was time to start up again. I used a different translation of the Bible, and I once again began to pray the Psalms. And I am praying just one Psalm per day, slowly, lingering with a few verses that seem to stick out to me a little more. It has been fresh.

(2) *Sacrifice*. Often, in order to get to your next level with God, that movement is going to require sacrifice. So, when I am plateaued, it is common for me to adjust my rhythm and to engage in some sacrificial acts in my pursuit of God. I've talked about this a great deal in other books like *Spiritual Authority, River Dwellers,* and *The Soul Care Leader,* so I won't spend much time with it here, only to mention that the three sacrificial acts I lean into the most are fasting (a sacrifice of food), watching (a sacrifice of sleep), and retreating (a sacrifice of time—giving God a longer block of time). If I get plateaued, my immediate reaction is to set aside a day to get alone to meet with God on a retreat and fast for that day.

This past year, 2024, was a year of tremendous loss for Jen and I. It began in January when my best friend, Martin Sanders, died unexpectedly. I spent an inordinate amount of time with Martin. His friendship and life were an immeasurable gift to me, and I miss him every day. Since then, we have lost two family members, along with three people who were leaders in the church that I pastored for more than twenty years, plus a pet dog, and another dear friend. When you go through a season of great loss it is draining on the soul, and you have less energy than normal. If you continue life without adjustments, you will burn out or hit a significant wall. So, this year, I have found that I need to guard my energy levels more than normal. This is part of making adjustments to my spiritual rhythm. When you have more drains on your soul, you need to adjust your rhythm. You need more inputs and less outputs.

This year I have been doing two spiritual retreats per month, instead of one, which had been my practice for many years. I have also taken on less appointments, answered less emails, spent less time doing ministry to individuals at conferences, and made some adjustments on both the inputs and outputs in my life to help navigate through the energy drain of a season of grief. I have also spent a lot more time processing sadness. I still feel love, joy, and peace every day, but it is intermingled with more sadness than usual, which can be expected. I have been sinking my roots deeper into my eternal citizenship because of the loss. We are truly just passing through. This is not my home; I am merely a stranger and alien here. My true citizenship is in Heaven, and grief reminds me of my true home.

I have also spent a lot more time processing sadness. I still feel love, joy, and peace every day, but it is intermingled with more sadness than usual, which can be expected.

Exercises

(1) **Examine your spiritual rhythm. What are you currently doing for spiritual practices? What are you doing daily, weekly, monthly, and yearly to draw near to God? Write down your current practices.** (I'll share mine here as an example, not for comparison.)

Daily: *Emptying*: pray through my to-do list; make sure my confessions are current; pray through my negative emotions. *Scripture intake:* meditation on a gospel passage; pray through at least one Psalm. Read through the Bible in a year. *Worship and thanksgiving:* today I soaked in some worship songs, and my heart was overflowing with thanksgiving for the goodness of God in my life. *Intercession and petition:* I pray for family and friends and pray through some of the promises God has given me. *Silence and listening:* I usually end my time with God in silence, fixing my loving attention on his presence, and I also spend time listening to the Spirit for anything He wants to say to me, or for any wisdom I might need from Him.

Weekly: I usually fast one day per week.

Monthly: I take at least one retreat day per month, though through this current year I have done two each month.

Yearly: Every summer I take a longer block of time off to pray, fast, and write.

Now write down your rhythm.

Daily:

Weekly:

Monthly:

Yearly:

(2) **Is your rhythm working? Do you love God and people more consistently in your life this year than two years ago? Is Jesus your first love and primary obsession? Is your rhythm leading you to greater freedom and fullness? At this time, are you growing closer to God? Do you feel free and full in Christ? Are you experiencing love, joy, and peace consistently? What spiritual disciplines are you engaged in that are fresh and vital? Are there any practices that have become old, stale, and tired for you?**

Journal some notes on the state of your current rhythm:

Do you need to make any adjustments to your rhythm? Ask the Spirit for insight. "Lord, what do I need to change? What could I do differently that would help me connect with you more? Is there any sacrifice you are calling me to engage in that would help my intimacy with you? Is there any spiritual practice I need to add to help me seek your face?"

Write some of your thoughts, prayers, and ideas here:

As you make adjustments to your rhythm, over the next couple of weeks monitor those adjustments and evaluate how the changes are working. Sometimes it takes only a couple of tweaks to your rhythm to adjust it and feel like you are connecting well with God.

(3) Are you seeking God's face? Or has too much of your time alone with God been about seeking his hands? Is God calling you to adjust your time with Him to spend more time seeking his face? What adjustments do you need to make? What disciplines do you need to engage in to seek his face?

List some of your thoughts and ideas here:

(4) **Schedule a day to take a larger block of time alone with God. If you have never done a spiritual retreat, you may want to take a half day to be alone with God. Jesus practiced spiritual retreats. He often withdrew to lonely places to pray and be alone with his Father. He often had to do it early in the morning, or in the middle of the night, because He was in such demand, but He made time for retreats. If Jesus, the sinless Son of God, needed to retreat, how much more the rest of us? Retreats are refueling centers for the soul. Nothing has helped me go deeper with God than the regular, consistent practice of spiritual retreats. I believe there are places of depth with God we cannot get to on a devotional diet. There are some deep places with God we can get to only with more lingering time in his presence.**

Here is some practical help on how to spend a retreat day with God.

- *Empty.* Pray through your to-do list. Make sure your confessions are current. Pray through any distracting or negative emotions.
- *Meditate on Scripture to turn your heart toward God.* You may pick a Psalm, a passage from the gospels, or another passage that God has led you to. Linger in the Word. Pay attention to the stirrings of the Spirit, the illumination, revelation, and convictions of the Spirit.
- *Worship.* Spend time worshiping, soaking in God's presence. Linger in his presence. Attend to his presence. *Don't rush.*
- *Silence.* What is God saying to you? When you empty your soul from all the distractions, your heart gets still, and you can more easily hear the still, small voice of the Spirit. Then just linger in silence fixing your loving attention on Jesus. If your mind wanders, simply bring it back to God gently with a phrase from Scripture that you were meditating on, or just speak Jesus' name.

I am including here something I practiced at the monastery. I call it "God-initiated conversations." It is another way to spend time alone with God and draw near to Him.

GOD-INITIATED CONVERSATIONS

Overview

Every deep relationship contains meaningful two-way conversations. If a conversation gets too one-sided, it becomes a monologue, and the relationship stagnates. Years ago, when I went to the monastery for extended blocks of time away with God, I began practicing something I called "God-initiated conversations." These took me to new places of depth and intimacy with God. Here is how my days would go (which I will place in present tense here to provide a real-time feel).

I arrive at the monastery where I rent a room for short retreats, getting there fairly early in the morning. I spend the morning alone with God. In the afternoon, I take a walk through the woods to the reservoir; I worship as I walk. I put on my earphones, and I sing out loud. The woods are always quiet, and no one else is there; it is a serene and peaceful walk. As I worship and focus my attention on God's presence, I take in the beauty of creation, and it brings joy and refreshment to my soul. When I get to the reservoir, I find a quiet spot to sit. I pray through the issues that are on my heart. Dreams. Desires. Concerns. Heartaches. Whatever is on my heart, I'll cry it out to God.

After I finish, I sit by the lake a little longer in silence. As I walk back, I don't listen to any music. I walk in complete silence. I don't initiate any conversation with God; I don't talk to Him about anything at all. I just avail myself completely to God and listen to *whatever is on His heart.* I cannot tell you how much this has increased my intimacy with God. Some of my sweetest, most intimate moments with the Father have occurred in these God-initiated conversations as God begins to share his heart with me.

I just avail myself completely to God and listen to *whatever is on His heart.* I cannot tell you how much this has increased my intimacy with God.

Now it's your turn to set aside time to hear from God.

Starting Your God-Initiated Conversation

First, take time to worship. I love taking a worship walk, but you can easily sit and worship. The issue is to fully engage. Worship ushers us into God's presence. Worship connects my heart to God. Worship reminds me of God's greatness and his affection for me. Sing. Shout. Break the stronghold of religion; give God his due honor. Worship wholeheartedly. I find that I need fresh music. Once I can sing a song and think about something else, it is hard for that song to touch my heart any longer. If I can't find new songs that touch my heart, then I pray the Psalms back to God in my own words.

Psalm 100:1-5: *"Shout for joy to the Lord, all the earth. Worship the Lord with gladness; come before him with joyful songs. Know that the Lord is God. It is he who made us, and we are his; we are his people, the sheep of his pasture. Enter his gates with thanksgiving and his courts with praise; give thanks to him and praise his name. For the Lord is good and his love endures forever; his faithfulness continues through all generations."*

Second, take time for surrender and confession if there is anything blocking your relationship with God.

Psalm 139:23, 24: *"Search me, God, and know my heart; test me and know my anxious thoughts. See if there is any offensive way in me, and lead me in the way everlasting."*

I want my soul to be still. This is part of the preparation. I want to cultivate an inner quiet, an inner stillness. Our soul is like a lake; if the lake of our souls is stormy, then it is hard to hear his still, small voice. Process the issues that are competing for your heart's affections and your heart's attention. Ask the Lord to show you if there is any sin that is unconfessed. Is there anyone you need to forgive? Is there any fear that is keeping you from peace and his presence? Notice that before David asks God to show him if there is any offensive way in him, he asks God to show him if there are any anxious thoughts. Let the Holy Spirit show you any barriers to inner stillness that can rob you of access to his presence.

Our soul is like a lake; if the lake of our souls is stormy, then it is hard to hear his still, small voice.

Third, meditation on Scripture can often prime the pump and prepare my heart for God-initiated conversations. Sometimes when I am at the monastery, I will meditate on Scripture when I am in the room before I leave. Other times I will meditate on Scripture by the lake. Here are some good meditative things to do.

Read the passage slowly. Read it out loud. Read it in multiple translations. (E.g., for one exercise that I did—Isaiah 40; 2 Corinthians 4—these were good passages to meditate on. You may pick a Psalm, like Psalm 63.) Read it several times. Read it slowly, out loud, with inflection. Sometimes I'll listen to it on my iPhone and let someone else read it to me, which can be helpful, because they will inflect things differently, and I'll see a passage in a fresh way.

Reflect on the passage. One of the Hebrew words for meditation is the word mumble. Mumble it, literally. Mutter the passage for a bit.

- What jumps out at you? What phrase? What word? What image?

- Where does the passage catch your heart?
- What does the Spirit illuminate or highlight for you? I try to pay attention to the Spirit's stirrings as I read the passage and linger there with Him.
- Why is this striking me? Why is the Spirit stirring within me as I read this section? Wait on God as He illuminates the passage. Linger with the passage in God's presence.

Pray the passage. Pray the passage back to God. Pray the passage into your life. Pray for insight. Pray for revelation. Often, going through a passage like this, I will come up with prophetic insight into the Word.

Fourth, pray through the issues on your heart. The first thing I pray through is my to-do list. These are often the things that are on my agenda that distract me from God's presence. I pray through all the distracting factors of my life. And I surrender them to God. Pray over any issues that are troubling you. Leave them with God. Deal with your fears. You want to be in a position of faith. Speak to God about the desires of your heart. I do this to clear the deck with God. I want to get all of the interference out of my soul so when it comes time to listen, I have nothing coming up, nothing interfering with God's presence and his voice. As far as possible, I want nothing blocking me or distracting me from Him. The goal is a quiet inner being, an inner stillness. Here are two helpful passages:

> **Philippians 4:4-7:** *"Rejoice in the Lord always. I will say it again: Rejoice! Let your gentleness be evident to all. The Lord is near. Do not be anxious about anything, but in every situation, by prayer and petition, with thanksgiving, present your requests to God. And the peace of God, which transcends all understanding, will guard your hearts and your minds in Christ Jesus."*
>
> Follow the passage. Do what it says. Praise. Gentleness is really about meekness, surrender. God is near. Let go of anxiety. With prayer, and thanksgiving, present your requests to God. Let peace come; it is a supernatural by-product of choosing to focus on his presence and surrender the issues of life to a loving Father.
>
> **1 Thessalonians 5:16-20:** *"Rejoice always, pray continually, give thanks in all circumstances; for this is God's will for you in Christ Jesus. Do not put out the Spirit's fire. Do not treat prophecies with contempt."*
>
> Rejoice always, give thanks in all circumstances; these are key to the cycle of renewal. They keep the fire burning so we can hear God's voice. Pray through, but do so with thanksgiving.

Fifth, let God speak. Now I am ready and prepared to wait in stillness. Usually, when I am at the monastery, I begin this stillness and waiting by the lake. I don't rush out of this time of prayer, petition, and thanksgiving. I linger in God's presence. I wait in silence. After a little while of stillness, I begin my walk home. I walk a little slower and fix my loving attention on his presence. Up until this point I've been offloading; I've been preparing my heart to meet with God, to hear his voice. Now I simply invite God to speak. Like the boy Samuel, I pray, "Speak, Lord, your servant listens." Then I begin my walk home, listening as I go. There is no background noise except the sounds of nature. I present no requests to God in this time. I initiate none of our conversation from this point forth. I've done my talking; now it is time to listen. I allow God to speak to me about whatever is on his mind. And I respond to what He initiates. He goes from topic to topic—just like a typical long-winding conversation between two friends. I respond to what He says, but I let Him lead me where He wants to take me.

Many of my most intimate conversations with God have occurred on these walks through the woods. I give God my full attention. My soul is prepared to hear. The pump is primed. And now I linger in the presence of God for an uninterrupted hour of God-initiated conversation. It is very free-flowing, like conversations with good friends. Random topics just pop up. One day while walking in the rain, I heard God whisper, "You know what I like about the rain?" For the next five to ten minutes, God talked to me about why He likes the rain.

One day the Lord said to me, "I whisper to you about the secrets of my heart." If we prepare our hearts and give Him an uninterrupted block of time, He will often reveal Himself to us. Sometimes He talks to me about my relationship with Jen, the kids, his plans for my life, or other things on his heart. But mostly, God and I are becoming friends because I linger in his presence and give him space to share his intimate thoughts with me. God doesn't need a friend. He has complete community in the Trinity. But God wants friends because He loves us. These God-initiated conversations have done more for my friendship with God than anything else. They have refreshed my spirit, renewed my soul.

Take the time to prepare your heart. Set aside a block of time with God. Off-load everything you can. And then just let God speak. I pray you will make it part of your regular journey with God!

Notes

Notes

Two

THE LIFE-CHANGE JOURNEY

Preparation work for this chapter:

In the *Soul Care* book, read the first two chapters (Introduction: My Journey to Soul Care, and Gateways to Life Change)

In the Video series, there is no corresponding video

In the Soul Care eCourse, watch lessons 1-5

My Journey to Soul Care

Jen and I planted a church in the Boston area back in 1995. The church was growing, and people were coming to Christ, but we hit a snag—Jen no longer liked me. In the beginning, probably pretty typically, I focused on Jen. She was the one who was upset, after all. So I prayed: "God fix her, change her, heal her. Whatever she needs." But I learned two incredibly important relational principles: (1) *It takes two healthy people to have a healthy relationship.* If, on a scale of 1 to 10, you are a 3 in terms of your spiritual and emotional health, the healthiest relationship you will ever have in that relationship is a 3. If you want that relationship to move from a 3 to 6, the only path to get there is . . . you must change. (2) *You cannot fix a relational problem by focusing on the other person's issues.* You are the only one responsible for you. The only chance you have to fix this relational problem is to become a healthier you and elevate the level of healthy interactions in your relationship.

Once I realized I needed to change, that led me to another problem: I didn't know how to change. Church hadn't taught me how to change; the people in church taught me how to *behave.* I was doing the things I was supposed to be doing, but I wasn't experiencing transformation. "You can't fix the problems of the soul with a change in behavior only" (*Soul Care: 7 Transformational Principles for a Healthy Soul,* Carpenter's Son Publishing, 2016, p.5). I needed Jesus to teach me how deep life change really works, and gratefully, He did.

Church hadn't taught me how to change; the people in church taught me how to *behave*.

I had to fight my base instinct to resist the Holy Spirit. Life change cannot occur when we are intentionally or unintentionally resisting the Holy Spirit. The first area of my resistance that God needed to address was my defensiveness. Jen and I started having conversations every night in an attempt to resolve the marriage conflict, and in the beginning the conversations would go like this: Jen would tell me what she was upset about, and I would defend myself. She didn't feel heard or listened to, and she ramped up her rhetoric, and I would defend myself again. We were in these emotionally escalating conversations every night, and we were getting nowhere. We weren't yelling or calling each other names, but the conversations were intense, and we were not making any progress.

One night I got alone with God and said, "Lord, you need to help us! We are struggling in our marriage. We are trying to talk it through, and we aren't getting anywhere." I heard the Lord in my inner being say, "Stop defending yourself. I don't want you to defend yourself anymore." I said, "That's one of my best tools, really." I sensed the Lord saying: "No, it isn't. Only insecure people defend themselves. And every time you defend yourself, you are resisting the light I offer you as a gift." I had to fight my base instinct to resist the Holy Spirit, so I laid down my right to defend myself. Please hear me: I still felt defensive, but I tried to listen for what Jen was saying without defending.

The conversations, though, felt so hopeless to both of us. Each night as we continued talking, Jen shared what she was upset about, I listened without defending, and I would say, "I hear you saying these things." Then I repeated back in my own words what I felt she was trying to say until she agreed that is what she meant. But I would often end these conversations by saying, with a sigh, "It's always my fault." This went on for a little while until one night I was praying and I heard the Lord say "Ephesians 5." I knew the passage: it is about husbands loving their wives. I read it and saw the line about how Jesus presented his bride blameless, and I heard the Lord whisper, "I present my bride blameless, but you are blaming yours." I realized that, once again, by blaming, I was resisting the Holy Spirit. I wasn't allowing Him to show me the things He needed to show me so I could *truly* change.

So I stopped defending and stopped blaming, but I had one more card to play: I started bargaining with God. I was emotionally exhausted. Every time Sunday rolled around, I would pray, "Lord, if you give me strength, I will stand and preach." The Lord would strengthen me, and I would preach, but then I would come home and collapse on the couch in emotional exhaustion. And another week of seemingly fruitlessly conflicted conversations would take place.

I started praying, "Lord, you have six months to change this situation, to heal our marriage, to fix this. If it doesn't get resolved in six months, I am going to have to resign. I can't keep doing this. I am just too tired." But after praying this way for a while, once again I heard God speak. He said, "The law of the harvest." I knew he was referring to Galatians 6, the passage that says a person reaps what they sow. And I heard the Lord say: "You are standing in a field of weeds. Your marriage is a field of weeds. You can blame Jen for it if you want; you can blame me for it if you want. But it is your field. You have been sowing weed seeds into your marriage—seeds of anger and selfishness. If you want to reap a new field, you have to sow different seed." And that was the day I stopped resisting the Holy Spirit. That was the day I started taking responsibility for my life. Listen: Jen had parts to the conflict too, but those weren't my responsibility. All God was trying to get me to do was take responsibility for my own life-change journey.

> "You will never rise above your level of self-awareness. The things we deny about ourselves are the very things that deny us from the fullness of God."

Authentic humility begins with honesty, it ends with responsibility, and somewhere in the middle is death to self. That is when we stop making life too much about us and we start making life more about God and others. We truly surrender to Jesus and begin to experience transformation. I told the Lord I would listen to learn, I wouldn't defend, I wouldn't blame, I wouldn't bargain, I would seek to give Him access to any and every area of my heart. And the life-change journey began in earnest. "You will never rise above your level of self-awareness. The things we deny about ourselves are the very things that deny us from the fullness of God" (*Soul Care*, 2016, p. 15).

The process of life change involved time alone with God, reading a lot of books that helped my self-awareness, and moving into open, honest, confessional community life. Life change isn't easy. It takes hard work; you have to do the work. You begin by fighting your base instinct to resist the Holy Spirit.

Gateways to Life Change

If we are new creatures in Christ (2 Corinthians 5:17), why do old habits and sinful patterns of behavior stick around? Sometimes it is because we are focused on sin management or behavior modification; we are not dealing with the root of the matter. Jesus said, "Out of the overflow of the heart the mouth speaks" (Matthew 12:34). He also said, "For out of the heart come evil thoughts, murder, adultery, sexual immorality, theft, false testimony, slander" (Matthew 15:19). If you want to kill a weed in your garden, you don't chop off the head, you have to pull it up by the roots. "You must get to these root issues in order to experience true transformation" (*Soul Care*, 2016, p. 20).

One of my favorite *Soul Care* questions is: "What's underneath that?" Why do you do what you do, think what you think, feel what you feel? What is driving that? Soul Care calls us to look at root issues; it invites us to deal with matters of the heart so we can experience true life change.

Discipleship is really just changing culture. We are changing culture from the culture of our origin to the culture of the Kingdom of God. When Kingdom culture clashes with my American culture, or my Northeast culture, or my Reimer culture, if I don't choose Kingdom culture, I'm not really a follower. Sometimes we are more American, or Canadian, or Australian, or Korean, then we are Kingdom citizens. Sometimes I am more loyal to my family culture than I am to the Kingdom. This is another reason why we must fight our base instinct to resist the Holy Spirit, because we are naturally resistant to things that differ from our culture of origin. Our culture is what is normal to us, and when something is introduced that is "abnormal," we naturally resist it. But when Kingdom culture clashes with my Reimer culture, if I choose my Reimer culture, I'm not really a follower. I am demonstrating that my loyalty to my family of origin is superior to my loyalty to Jesus. This is why Jesus said that if we don't hate our mother and father, we cannot follow Him. He doesn't want us to literally *hate* our mothers; He is simply saying that our loyalty to Him must supersede all other loyalties in our life.

The Kingdom of God is a deep life-change culture, and there are certain elements of that culture that are essential for our transformation. But sometimes these things are not normal to us. Let me talk about three components of deep life change in Kingdom culture.

First, *life change involves anointed teaching.* I do not mean that the teacher is a gifted teacher; I am assuming gifting. When I say anointed teaching, I mean that the teacher has lived out that which they are proclaiming. They have integrated these teachings. This welcomes God's presence upon the teaching. Jesus is the anointed one, in part because He fully lived out every word He ever spoke. There is no discontinuance between what Jesus says and what Jesus does. Therefore, there is no hindrance to the flow of the Spirit in Jesus' life; every word He ever spoke is saturated with the presence of God. They are anointed words. When we live out the message we proclaim, it welcomes God's presence and anointing in a way that makes our words weighty, and we carry authority. We only have authority over that which we walk in victory. This creates an atmosphere of life-change potential, an atmosphere of breakthrough for those who have ears to hear and eyes to see. This is why it is important that you read the book *Soul Care* and/or listen to the Soul Care Videos and/or the Soul Care eCourse as you go through this. Listen and fight your base instinct to resist the Holy Spirit. It is essential to life change.

We have to live in open, honest, confessional community if we want to experience transformation.

Second, *life-change culture involves true community.* We have to live in open, honest, confessional community if we want to experience transformation. The triune God—the Trinity—has lived in the light with one another for all eternity. They have had no darkness between them, no sin within them, no divisions, no factions. They have lived in the light, in perfect harmony together for all eternity. We were created in the image of God; therefore, we were created for true community. The kingdom of Satan is a kingdom of darkness. It invites us into secrecy, hiding, lying, divisions, factions, and sin. We have to choose to be children of the light.

Think about the apostles. The greatest argument the apostles had throughout the gospels was about who was the greatest. Doesn't that give you hope? These guys went on to change the world, and they were so selfish and petty that they were constantly arguing over which of them was the greatest. But how do you know that this was their greatest argument? Because they told you! They had become children of the light. Listen, no one writing during this time was as open and honest about their sins, flaws, selfishness, and pettiness as were the apostles. But they had heard Jesus talk about the Kingdom of light, and they had become children of the light.

Part of finding freedom in my life was being honest. I struggled with lust, but I had never talked about it. I had grown up in a church that didn't talk openly about sex. I was struggling with lust, but I wanted to be a man of God. I had surrendered my life to Christ when I was 19, and I went to a Christian college. One night I took a risk and told a friend that I was struggling with lust. It was the first time I had ever been honest about it. It was the beginning of victory. Light always dispels darkness. We must choose to be children of the light. Later, when Jen and I were in that first marriage struggle, I was struggling with lust again, and I had to be honest with Jen, which helped me live in victory.

I want to urge you to walk through this workbook with someone else or a group of three (a triad). When I do Soul Care Conferences, or when I teach Soul Care in a seminary atmosphere, I don't just do teaching. I also have people break into small groups of three to discuss these principles and process them together. I invite people to live as children of the light. One of the reasons Soul Care has helped so many people find freedom in Christ is because of this call to true community. Now, I know some of you have been deeply hurt by community—by your family, by the church. When you have been hurt by community, you cannot be healed except in community. God will only take you so far in the healing process before He invites you back into a grace-filled community to help you discover healing. So find someone that you have some level of trust with, open up a little bit, see if they are honorable. If so, open up some more; if they continue to be honorable and loving without judgment, then invite them to journey with you through these principles and live together as children of the light. There is freedom in the light.

Third, *true life change always accesses the presence and power of God.* Only God can change the heart; only God can heal the soul. We need more than a theology of God's presence and power; we need to experience God's presence and power to be transformed. When I look back at my own life-change journey, at every turning point I can see evidence of the presence and power of God. God spoke to me, revealed Himself to me, encountered me, or filled me afresh. In some way, I met

God, and it left me different. This is why I began this book with the chapter on intimacy. We have to develop a rhythm that is keeping us vitally connected to Jesus —because only in Jesus' presence is there true freedom and fullness.

Throughout this workbook, I will call you to pause and listen for God's revelation and illumination. I will invite you to meditate on Scripture and allow the Holy Spirit to bring insight and wisdom. I will create opportunities for you to encounter the living God. Jesus is the same as He has always been (Hebrews 13:8); He hasn't changed. So Jesus can meet you like He met the Apostle Paul, like He met Mary Magdalene, and like He met countless others along the way in the New Testament. This is where life change so often begins—in the presence of Jesus, the risen One.

God never shines light into your heart and soul to make you feel bad; God shines light to get you free.

As you go through this workbook and do the hard work of the soul, God may give you dreams. Write them down. He may bring to mind memories that you have forgotten or repressed. Don't ignore those. God never brings things to light to hurt us. He only brings things into the light to heal us.

Sometimes people are afraid of the Holy Spirit. They are afraid of God's power or afraid of certain manifestations. It could have come from a bad church experience, and you find yourself a little fearful. But I want to remind you of an important truth: Jesus isn't afraid of the Holy Spirit. Fear of the Holy Spirit is demonic; it is a tool of the enemy to keep us from freedom and fullness. You don't need to be afraid of the Spirit's presence and power.

Sometimes we use the phrase, "What you don't know won't hurt you." But that isn't true. When it comes to the issues of your soul, what you don't know is killing you, and it is killing those around you. God never shines light into your heart and soul to make you feel bad; God shines light to get you free. You must fight your base instinct to resist the Holy Spirit and welcome the light of God as you work through things. May God bless you as you go!

As you go through this list of experiences (given below), do not rush. Do not feel like you need to do them all at once. As a matter of fact, it may be far more beneficial to walk through them slowly over many days, weeks, or even months for some issues that we struggle with. Pray, reflect, journal, process, and dialogue with your small group about these things. The goal is life change; we are seeking to integrate the freedom and fullness that is ours in Christ, not simply filling out a workbook.

Experiences

If you are going through this in a small group, break into groups of three and tell your story to one another. When you tell your story, be honest. Don't give the cleaned-up, nice Christian version: "Once I was blind, but now I see." Tell the real story. You may want to take an entire session on this exercise, or get together outside of your normal gathering and share your story together over a meal. Here are some thoughts to help guide you as you tell your story.

- Think of your story on a continuum, from the time you were born until your current age. What were some of your highs and lows on the journey? Peaks and valleys? Often these are formational times.
- Talk about your relationships with significant people—your family of origin, Mom, Dad, siblings. What were those relationships like?
- Use five to seven adjectives describing your parents/guardians. (Note: if they are all good, you are probably not living in reality! Likewise, if they are all bad, there are surely some positive adjectives you can find.)
- Talk about your painful points, your hurts and wounds in life. Some of those occurred at home, others in your neighborhoods, schools, marriage, and more.
- Tell about your spiritual encounters—this includes how you came to faith in Christ and had significant encounters with God. But it also includes encounters with dark spirits.
- What are some of the family slogans you grew up with? Some of them were spoken, some unspoken. For example, some of you were sworn to secrecy; you were forbidden to tell about something in your family, like abuse. These slogans often become like the "10 commandments" of our homes. Frequently, they are not in alignment with the Kingdom of light.
- Speak of some of the tragedies and losses you have experienced. For example, perhaps your Mom died when you were young. It wasn't anyone's fault, but it has shaped you.
- Write down some of your story in the bullet points below. (Throughout this workbook, I've purposefully left room to write for these exercises.)

(1) What do you need to unpack from the suitcase of your soul? Take a moment and invite the Lord to show you, and write some thoughts down. Where are you stuck and need freedom?

(2) If you are to rate your emotional and spiritual health on a scale of 1-10, where would you rate yourself? Be honest. God loves you wherever you are, but life change begins with honesty. What thoughts come to mind as you do this?

(3) How have you resisted the Holy Spirit? Where have you been defensive? What are you defensive about? Are there any areas where you blame others? Are you attempting to bargain with God? Pay close attention to when you resist the Holy Spirit over the next several days and jot down any place where you feel or display resistance. What are you resistant about? How do you show resistance?

(4) Authentic humility begins with honesty, ends with responsibility, and, somewhere in the middle, is death to self. When we die to self, we stop making it too much about us and begin to make it more about Jesus and others. Slow down. Quiet your heart before the Lord and ask Him for insight as you process these questions. If you are doing this with others, you may want to take time to share your discoveries. Are there areas where you are not being honest with yourself and others? Is God calling you to humble yourself in some area of your life? Have you been resisting the Holy Spirit? Sometimes the way we resist the Holy Spirit is with our hiddenness; we sense God calling us to be honest, but we refuse. Are there any areas where you have been making excuses and not taking responsibility for your life? Is God

calling you to take responsibility for some area where you have been shirking responsibility or blaming others? Jesus told us to pick up our cross daily and follow Him. Where is Jesus asking you to take up your cross? Where is Jesus calling you to die to your self-life?

(5) Privatized religion produces shame and bondage. "There is no transformation without confession. There is no victory in hiding. There is no breakthrough in secrecy" (*Soul Care*, 2016, p. 27). How does guilt and shame show up in your life? Do you sense that you need to confess something to someone to move toward greater freedom and transformation in your life? If so, what do you need to bring into the light? Who do you need to process with?

(6) Do you have any areas of your life where you feel stuck? This is a behavior, attitude, sin, or dysfunction where you have not been able to find breakthrough. What is that area? Take time to reflect with God about it. What is underneath that area? Why do you do what you do, think what you think, feel what you feel in that area? Ask the Lord to show you the roots. How might it be connected to your story? What could be some of the heart and soul issues that need to be addressed?

(7) When have you felt hopeless to change a destructive behavior in your life? How did you attempt sin management? What was the result?

(8) Where does your family culture, or country culture, or region-of-origin culture clash with the culture of God's Kingdom in your life? Personalize it, but don't make it a cultural critique or family critique. Engage with this exercise to bring yourself into alignment with Jesus' culture. Linger with the question and ask the Holy Spirit for insight.

(9) As you read these chapters in *Soul Care*, and/or listen to the Videos/eCourse, are there any places where you find yourself resistant to the teaching? Are there any new insights that have come to you, fresh revelations you have received as you have read or listened?

(10) The Bible calls us to live in the light with God and others (1 John 1). Are there areas where, in truth, you are in the darkness? Do you have a couple of people in your life you are completely honest with? What do you find most difficult about the concept of being completely honest with others? What fears does it trigger within you? Does it bring up shame?

(11) How have you experienced God's presence and power in your life? Have you experienced any fear of the Spirit's presence, power, or manifestations? Where does that come from? Where do you need God's presence and power, right now, in your life?

Notes

Notes

Three

IDENTITY: OVERCOMING LIES

Preparation work for this chapter:

Read "Soul Care Principle #1: Identity" in the *Soul Care* book

In the Video series, watch the video on "Overcoming Lies"

In the Soul Care eCourse, watch lessons 6-10

Summary of Soul Care Principle #1: Identity

Think of your identity like the foundation of a building. If the foundation of a building is not properly set, no matter how good the building material, no matter how good the builder, the building is in jeopardy. "What you believe about yourself is the foundation of your life; it is your identity, and a faulty foundation will create cracks in the soul" (*Soul Care*, 2016, pp. 35, 36).

In the New Testament, the authors frequently say that we are "in Christ" and Christ is "in us." We are united with Christ; we have been chosen, adopted, and we are deeply loved children of God. The problem, for many of us, isn't that we don't know these truths. I might ask you, "Do you know that God loves you?" You would likely tell me yes and know some Bible verses to make that point. But the question isn't merely, "Do you know you are loved by God?" The question is: "Are you living like a deeply loved person in all of your human interactions?" That's the real question. When we live like a deeply loved person, we have solidified our identity. James tells us that faith without deeds is dead (James 2:26). If you know you are loved by God but you are still living like an unloved, insecure person, your faith isn't impacting the way you live your life.

We need to learn to integrate the truth about our identity in our daily lives so that we live like deeply loved children of God. Victory starts with self-awareness. We have to recognize the lies we believe are preventing us from living like deeply loved children of God. "The power of a lie is in our agreement with it. Whatever we agree with, we give power to. If you agree with the truth, and hold on to the truth, the truth will set you free, but if you agree with a lie, its influence will cast a shadow in your life" (*Soul Care,* 2016, p. 39).

To overcome the lies that we believe, we must renew our minds (Romans 12:2). Jesus said, "If you hold to my teaching, you are really my disciples. Then you will know the truth, and the truth will set you free" (John 8:31, 32). People often misquote this passage by quoting only the second half of the verse, but it is an *if/then* promise. Jesus didn't teach that the truth will set you free. Jesus said: if we hold to his teaching, then we will know the truth, and the truth will set us free. We have to hold on to the teaching of who we are in Christ precisely when someone is challenging that by their behaviors, words, or attitudes toward us. We must hold to the fact that we are deeply loved by God even when, for instance, our spouse doesn't love us anymore. We have to hold to the fact that we are loved by God when our boss is angry at us and demotes us. Can we live like deeply loved children of God when the people around us are not loving us?

All of us have been impacted by lies; these are a by-product of living life in a fallen world. Lies form in us as a result of things we have been told, things that are done to us, pains and heartaches we have experienced, the culture we live in, our own sin, and Satan's evil influence. We can't live free and full in Christ unless we identify these lies and renew our minds with the truth of who we are in Christ.

The process of freedom begins with self-awareness, so we must discover these lies that we have come to believe. David Benner, in his book *The Gift of Being Yourself,* says that our false self often reaches for "fig leaves" just as Adam and Eve did to cover our sense of inadequacy and shame. Our fig leaves are just more sophisticated than those of our earliest ancestors. Let's look at some of the symptoms of the lies we believe.

First, *when we are standing on a shaky foundation, rather than relying on the truth of who we are in Christ, we often become defensive.* I mentioned earlier that the Lord told me not to defend myself anymore because only insecure people are defensive. When I realized that Jen was upset with me, I asked her what she was upset about. But every time she tried to tell me something, I defended myself. It was revealing the lie I believed—that I needed Jen to love me to somehow validate me, and that when Jen disagreed with me or didn't like me, I felt invalidated.

Secure people don't defend themselves. Jesus never defended Himself. In 1 Peter 2, Peter is talking to a church in suffering, and he essentially tells them that if they suffer for living righteous lives, God will reward them. But if they suffer for wrongdoing, then they get what they deserve. In that context, Peter wants to encourage those who are suffering for godly living, and he tells them that Jesus suffered even though He never sinned and never did wrong. He writes, "To this you were called [to suffer for godly living], because Christ suffered for you, leaving you an example, that you should follow in his steps. 'He committed no sin, and no deceit was found in his mouth'" (1 Peter 2:21, 22). Jesus didn't sin; therefore, Jesus never suffered because of any wrongful deeds. Jesus never spoke any lies, or said anything with malice, so Jesus never suffered because of wrongful words.

Yet Jesus suffered, and look at how He responds: "When they hurled their insults at him, he did not retaliate; when he suffered, he made no threats" (1 Peter 2:23). Jesus didn't counterattack; Jesus didn't defend Himself. Jesus didn't retaliate, threaten, cajole, or control in the face of suffering. How was He able to respond without power and defensiveness? "Instead, he entrusted himself to him who judges justly" (1 Peter 2:23). Jesus did not entrust Himself to what people said about Him or thought about Him. Jesus recognized that people's opinions were temporal and often false. Jesus entrusted Himself to what his Father thought and said about Him. The Father's opinion was eternal and always true. The Father had already spoken both at Jesus' baptism and transfiguration; the Father had said that this was his Son, whom He loved, and with Jesus He was well pleased. That is the Father's verdict. Therefore, because Jesus didn't put stock in other verdicts, He did not need to defend Himself. The Father had spoken, and Jesus trusted the Father's word about Him. When we are defensive it reveals that we are gaining our identity in the temporal rather than the eternal; we are trusting other opinions over the Father's opinion.

So what are you defensive about? If you really don't know, go ask a few people close to you. Say, "If I were to be defensive, what might I be defensive about?" And when they tell you, don't defend yourself!

Second, *pettiness is another symptom that reveals the lies you believe.* What annoys you about other people often points to an area where you gain some sense of worth or value. For example, if you are annoyed with lazy people, it is likely because you gain some value from your performance. What do you find annoying about other people? It likely indicates more about you than it does about the other person. Why do you find that person annoying? What does it reveal to you about where you are gaining a sense of worth, value, or significance? Often, we just assume our thoughts, opinions, and feelings are right, and the other person is wrong, and we don't examine ourselves. Dig deeper. Look inside. Why are you bothered by that? Where does it indicate a lie about your value that you believe?

What do you find annoying about other people? It likely indicates more about you than it does about the other person. Why do you find that person annoying?

Third, *our compulsiveness often points to our false ways of being.* We are compulsive about things we have some deprivation in. We sense this empty void in our souls, and we become compulsive about something in order to cover up the lie that is underneath the deprivation. For example, the root of addiction is shame. We have this lie inside that says: "I am not lovable. I don't have what it takes to succeed." It makes us feel bad, so we reach for something that brings us comfort, like alcohol, and then we feel a little better when we drink. But then the effect of the alcohol wears off, and that old feeling comes back, so we reach for it again—and again, and again—to cover up the lie we believe: "Something is wrong with me; I'm not lovable; I don't have what it takes."

If we are going to get free from the symptoms that lies create, we have to identify the lies and pluck them out by the roots. We have to figure out where the lies are formed. What were the things said to us, the things done to us, the things we have done and said to ourselves that formed the lies in us? In the section below, I will give you some specific exercises to participate in to help you. If you want to get well, to experience freedom and fullness in Christ, then do the work. Don't just read it.

For me, the greatest indicator that I was standing on the false foundation of a lie was that I lost my peace; I started feeling uneasy and anxious inside. It wasn't overwhelming, but I had lost the peace of Christ. For example, when I first start wrestling with these things, I pay really close attention to my self-talk. What do you say to yourself, about yourself? What are the imaginary conversations you have with others in your head? When I was a young pastor, I began to notice that if someone came to me on a Sunday morning after church and said, "I need to talk to you," I would begin to entertain thoughts in my head that were not rooted in security. I would set an appointment with the person and then I would go home after church and my mind would start buzzing. "What did I say to Joe that he wants to meet with me? I don't remember saying anything to him that would have offended him. What is Joe upset about? Well, there was that one thing I said, but I didn't mean anything by that. I can't believe he took offense at that." And I would have this conversation in my head with Joe. I would think about what I was going to say, what he was going to say, how I would respond, and by the end of the conversation Joe would be on his knees in repentance like he should be! But so often, when I got to the appointment with Joe, he would actually say something like this: "I'm really struggling with my marriage, and I wanted you to help me." I would think, *I'm not helping you! You just wasted three days of my life!* But the reality is Joe didn't waste any of my life. When you have undealt-with issues in your soul, you waste untold amounts of emotional energy in your head. That which runs through your head unfiltered reveals that which is undealt with in your heart. Pay attention to your self-talk; it is a major clue to the lies you believe!

Secure people don't have imaginary conversations with people; they just deal with the issue directly and lovingly.

Imaginary conversations have become illegal for me. I realized that the only time I had an imaginary conversation with someone was when I was wrestling with insecurity; I was standing on a false foundation. Secure people don't have imaginary conversations with people; they just deal with the issue directly and lovingly.

There are three core lies that people believe. There are many variations of these lies, but these are the big three. All the identity lies impact the sense of our value. We feel as though our value is dependent on something other than the love of God. We know that this isn't true, but it feels true and we are acting like it is true.

The first lie: *the issue of my value is dependent on my performance.* I feel like I am worthy and valuable when my performance is up to snuff. It may be moral performance: I feel good about myself if I am doing all the things I am supposed to be doing, and not doing the wrong things. Then one day I fall into an old besetting sin pattern, and I feel like I need to crawl across glass to get back to God; that is the performance lie. "God only loves me if I get my act together." "People will only accept me if I behave properly." If you get a performance review at work and you get five positive comments and one negative comment, what do you go home and focus on? If you go home and focus on the negative comment, that is indicative of the performance lie.

Second lie: *the issue of my value is dependent on whether certain people love me.* For some of us, we don't need everyone to love us, just "almost everyone"! For others of us, it is important people: family, certain friends, people in authority. For me, I didn't need everyone to love me, but when Jen didn't love me, that exposed the reality of this lie in my soul. I was anxious, upset, obsessed with repairing the relationship and changing Jen's opinion about me—all because I felt my worth was tied to what Jen thought about me. I had to get to the place where I realized that life was better when Jen liked me, and I wanted Jen to like me, but even if Jen didn't like me, I was going to be okay, because Jesus loved me and that was enough for me. "If you believe the lie that you need people's approval to feel good about yourself, then you will feel anxiety when people are upset with [you]. You will get defensive and hurt by criticism" (*Soul Care,* 2016, p. 55).

Do you think Jesus went home at night and couldn't sleep because of the criticism He received from the Pharisees? Or because his disciples were upset with Him? No. Jesus was secure in his Father's opinion.

Third, *the issue of my value is dependent on whether I am in control.* Listen: if someone has told you that you are controlling, it is likely because you are to some degree. It doesn't do any good to defend yourself; instead, try to gain understanding. Ask people sincerely: "What do I do that makes you feel controlled? Why do you say that I am controlling? How does it show up?" Don't ask to defend, ask to gain self-awareness. For some of you, the people around you feel controlled by you. That isn't the person you want to be. Defending yourself will never change that behavior. For others, the people around you don't feel controlled, but you want to control outcomes, and if you can't control outcomes, you feel angry or maybe even a little depressed.

All three of these lies have impacted my life. The one that *should* have the most influence in my life, based on my personality, is the control lie. People around me do not usually feel controlled by me, but when I cannot control an outcome, it has often caused me to be irritated and aggravated.

But the lie that has had the greatest influence on my life is the people-pleasing lie, and that is because of my wounding. Your wounding often trumps your personality. This is one of the reasons you have to look beyond personality profiles; they often don't tell the whole story.

Here is the truth: the issue of my value is settled at the cross. On the cross of Jesus Christ, the Father spoke over our lives and said, "I love you so much. I found you worthy of my Son's blood." That is the Father's estimation of your worth. I had to get to the place where I realized that even if Jen didn't love me, even if Jen left me, the issue of my value was settled at the cross. The Father loved me, and that is enough for my well-being. I knew these things to be true, but I wasn't living like a deeply loved person. That was part of the reason we were struggling in our marriage. I had to start living like a deeply loved person in all of our relational interactions.

So how do we shift from this false platform to the true foundation of God's love? How do we live in all of life's circumstances, and all of our human interactions, like deeply loved children of God?

First, *we have to identify the lies and their manifestations.* What lie has the greatest influence in your life? When you are standing on that lie, what are the manifestations? To determine the manifestations of a lie, ask these three questions: (1) What do you think? What runs through your head when you are standing on the lie? (2) What do you feel? What do you feel viscerally, physically, emotionally when you are standing on that lie? (3) How do you behave? How do you act when you are standing on that lie? Let me answer these in my life, as an example, as you think about your own life.

The lie that has had the most hold on me is the people-pleasing lie: the issue of my value is dependent on what others think, especially my wife Jen. (1) What do I think when I am standing on that false foundation? My mind is racing; I can't shut it down. I am tempted to have imaginary conversations with the person in my head: justifying myself, defending myself, "winning the person over." (2) What do I feel? I lose my peace; I feel low buzzing anxiety in my heart and soul. My chest tightens a bit, my heart races, and I am robbed of my peace. I often feel defensive, hurt, and angry. I want to prove myself, defend myself, protect myself. (3) How do I behave? If I am hurt, I feel a desire to withdraw from the person: not necessarily physically, but at least emotionally. To pull back and protect myself rather than relying on Jesus' love to be my shield and protection. When I feel threatened, I am much more likely to feel defensive and go on the counterattack. These manifestations are our indicator clues that we are standing on the false foundation, that we need to renew our mind.

Second, *to move from the false foundation to the true foundation of God's love, we have to renew our minds.* Recognize when you are standing on the false foundation and reposition the issue of your value in Christ. This is when you "hold on" to the truth or "renew your mind." In the early days when Jen and I were having these marriage struggles, because of the Spirit's direction, I stopped defending myself. I would still feel defensive, but I would listen without defending, and then I would go upstairs alone with God and renew my mind. I would say, "I want Jen to like me; life is better when Jen likes me. But even if Jen doesn't like me, Jesus loves me, and that is enough for me. I've been chosen before the foundations of the earth; I am a deeply loved, adopted child of God. The issue of my value was settled at the cross." I told myself the truth and held on to that rather than allowing the lie to cause me to cascade off into imaginary conversations.

Third, *to change from the false foundation to the true foundation of who we are in Christ, we need to allow the Holy Spirit to reveal the love of God to us.* Paul says in Romans 8:16, "The Spirit testifies with our spirit that we are God's children." We need to listen to the testimony of the Holy Spirit. So I would sit alone with God after these painful conversations and I would renew my mind, and this would help slow my angst, and then I would simply wait on God and ask the Lord to tell me what He thought. He would testify to me about the Father's love. The Father's love is not dependent on whether you get your act together or whether your family loves you. I would hear, every night, "I love you," and my heart would settle in the revelation of God's love.

Finally, if you want to change from the false foundation of lies to the truth that you are loved by God, *you have to act in courage as a deeply loved child of God.* Faith without deeds is dead. It doesn't do you any good if you tell yourself the truth but still act like an insecure, unloved person. If you want the truth to sink deep into your soul, you have to act on the truth. The more you act like a deeply loved person, the more you will feel deeply loved, and the more freedom you will experience. So I would end all of these sessions with God by asking, "How would a deeply loved person act right now?" A deeply loved person would own their part, so I asked the Lord, "What of these things that Jen told me is true?" Whatever the Lord told me was true. I would own those things with Jen and say to her, "The Lord showed me that is true about me. That is not the man I want to be. I give you permission to call me on that if I do it again."

The more you act like a deeply loved person, the more you will feel deeply loved, and the more freedom you will experience.

There are two special cases I want to look at that often impede us from solidifying our identity in Christ. First, *sometimes we have an identity wound.* Think of your identity like a bucket—an identity wound is like having a hole in the bottom of the bucket. Whatever you pour into the bucket just leaks out. It feels like nothing sticks, and there is an inner emptiness inside. You can have loving encounters with God and people, but it doesn't seem to take hold because of the hole in the identity. This requires a little extra attention to close the hole, heal the wound, and repair the identity. I have done a talk on healing identity wounds which is available on our website on Vimeo on Demand. You can also access it at this link: https://vimeo.com/user110103313/vod_pages .

The second identity issue that sometimes requires special attention is *the bent will.* If someone grows up with abuse, or bullying, or a highly controlling atmosphere, they will often develop a bent will. They feel powerless to change and overcome in life. The reality, however, is you may have been victimized, but you are *not* a victim—not as a Christian you aren't. This is because you are in Christ and Christ is not a victim. Jesus too was victimized, but Jesus overcame, and you are in Christ and have Christ in you, so you too can overcome (Romans 8:28-39). But you have to change the victim mentality that leaves you feeling powerless to overcome. I have done a sermon on overcoming toxic shame; it is available on our website, and you can listen and find a great deal to help you.

Again, take your time through the exercises that follow. You may only want to do one per day. Pray, think, reflect, and ask the Lord for insight as you take time considering these questions or participating in the exercises.

Experiences

(1) Of the three major lies (people-pleasing, performance, and control), which has the most influence on your life? What is the dominant lie you believe? Work through the four steps outlined above: (1) Identify the lie and its manifestations. What are the manifestations of the identity lies you believe? When the lie is influencing you, consider: what do you think? What do you feel? How do you act? Once we learn how we think, feel, and act from a lie, these symptoms become our indicator clues to turn to God and hold to the truth of who we are in Christ. (2) Replace the lie with the truth. Renew your mind and hold to the truth. You may want to memorize a Scripture that counteracts the lie you believe and use it whenever a symptom shows up. You also need to intentionally change your self-talk. (3) Every day, sit with the Holy Spirit and listen for what He wants to tell you. The Spirit testifies that we are dearly loved children of God (Romans 8:15, 16). Listen to and receive the testimony of the Holy Spirit. (4) Act like a deeply loved person. How would a deeply loved person act right now? Faith without deeds is dead.

(2) How has the people-pleasing lie impacted your life? What symptoms do you see of people-pleasing in you? What do you get defensive about? Are there times in your life when you feel people take advantage of you, and you begin to feel resentful? Is it hard for you to say no? Does it make you anxious when people are upset with you?

(3) How has the performance lie impacted your life? What are some of the symptoms of the performance lie in you? How did it get formed in you?

(4) How is control an issue in your life? Have people ever told you that you are controlling? When you are not in control, or feel out of control, how does it make you feel? Anxious, angry, worried, fearful, depressed?

(5) Tie the lies to your story. How did they get formed in you? Journal below on the following questions: what were some of the things that important people in your life said to you that contributed to this lie? What were some of the family slogans or sayings that were communicated that contributed to this lie? What were some of the actions, events, or shaping experiences that formed this lie in you? Pay close attention to repeat experiences because things that occur multiple times often form lies.

(6) Pay attention to your self-talk. What do you say to yourself, about yourself? What are the imaginary conversations you have in your head with others? What do those things reveal to you about the lies you believe? When do you find yourself tempted to engage in this self-talk? Are there specific events that trigger it? Don't allow yourself to keep going there. When these things come to your mind, this is when you must hold to the truth, do the identity work, and act like a deeply loved person.

(7) What are some of the indicator clues that you are standing on a false foundation? What are you most likely to be defensive about? Get help, if you need to, from those around you. What do you find annoying about other people? When do you become a little petty? What are you compulsive about? What do these things reveal to you about the lies you believe? Which symptoms do you recognize most in your life? When and how does it manifest? What causes you to doubt your sense of worth or feel insecure about yourself?

(8) What most often robs you of peace? When I (Rob) am standing on a lie, I lose my peace. This is one of the common indicators that we are standing on a lie. People speak of performance anxiety, for example. In what areas of your life are you currently experiencing anxiety? How is it connected to your identity? What causes you to lose your peace? What does that tell you about the lies you believe? How can you hold to the truth in those circumstances and renew your mind? What triggers you? Why? What is underneath that?

(9) Are you wrestling with either an identity wound—a hole in the bucket of your soul—or a bent will? What was (are) the wound(s)? How did the hole form in you? Do you have any symptoms of the bent will? Do you feel powerless at times? When? What makes you feel most vulnerable? Where do you blame others in your life? Where do you still hold on to shame? What can you do to go after that?

(10) Are you living like a deeply loved person in all of life's circumstances and all of your human interactions? When do you find yourself living like an unloved, insecure person? What patterns do you observe in your life around those insecure moments? What do they have in common?

(11) Meditate on Scriptures about your identity. You might want to begin by meditating on Ephesians chapters 1-3 over the next couple of weeks. In my book *Pathways to the King*, in Chapter 1: "Personalize Our Identity," I talk about three ways to meditate. First, is *lectio divina,* which is Latin for "divine reading." Read a passage about your identity in Christ (I will list several below) multiple times; you may read it in several translations. Ask the Holy Spirit for insight. What words, phrases, or images stand out to you as you read? Where do you sense the Holy Spirit stirring your soul? Linger in that place. Pray over the passage and what you sense God is showing you. Dialogue with Him about the passage and let Him speak to you on these issues and make them personal to you. Second, we can meditate on a passage by putting ourselves in the passage. If it is a narrative, try to imagine being there: see the sights, smell the smells, hear the sounds, feel the emotions. Ask the Holy Spirit to reveal Himself to you again. If it is a passage like Ephesians 1, read your name into the passage. Personalize it as you read. Third, you may want to write a passage down on an index card, prayer journal, or on a notes page in your phone. Read the passage slowly in the morning, asking God for revelation. Linger with the text. Read over it again at lunch, dinner, and bedtime. Allow the Holy Spirit to bring it to mind through the day, and as insights come to your mind, take a moment to jot them down on that card or on the phone note page. Second Timothy 3:16 says that all Scripture is God-breathed. Let the Holy Spirit reveal the truth of the passage to you personally. Jot down your insights. Below are some

passages about our identity that you can meditate on over days, weeks, months, and years to sink these truths deeper into your soul. Some of these passages you may want to linger with every day for months because the Holy Spirit is ministering to you through them. The goal is not merely to *know* the truth; the goal is to *live* like a deeply loved person.

- Ephesians 1:1-10. (A further example of meditation on this first passage: sometimes I will begin with a passage like this, and the Spirit breathes on the first verse: "God's holy people." That phrase stirs something in me. So I may not get any further than that one phrase for that day. I linger with it, pray about it, allow the Spirit to show me things. Then tomorrow I pick up where I left off.) I may meditate on a passage as rich as this one for weeks because the Spirit is taking it deeper. The goal of meditation is not knowledge, it is revelation. We want to linger with the text, hear from the Spirit in the Word, and personalize it.
- Ephesians 1:11—14
- Ephesians 1:15-23
- Ephesians 2:1-10
- Ephesians 2:11-22
- Ephesians 3:14-21
- Romans 8:1-13
- Romans 8:14-16
- Romans 8:28-30
- Romans 8:31-39
- Galatians 2:19-21
- Galatians 3:23-4:7
- Philippians 2:1-11
- Philippians 3:1-14
- Colossians 1:9-14
- Colossians 2:9-15
- Colossians 3:1-4

(12)I have written about our identity in Christ in *Pathways to the King* and *Spiritual Authority.* You may want to read through the chapters in those books as you are taking your identity deeper in Christ. You may also want to check out *The Gift of Being Yourself* by David Benner.

(13) Get alone with God. Empty yourself of your concerns. Pray through your to-do list; make sure your confessions are current. Pray through your negative emotions—whatever fears, anxieties, and hurts surface. After emptying, sit quietly with God. Ask the Holy Spirit to reveal what He thinks and feels about you. Don't analyze it: "Is that God? Is that me? How can I tell? I'm not sure." Don't live with introspection in your head, but learn to live by faith, receiving from the Spirit what He is saying. Romans 8:14-16 tells us that the Holy Spirit testifies to us that we are children of God. Listen for the testimony of the Spirit and write down what you sense God saying to you. Is it consistent with the Scriptures that speak of your identity in Christ? Receive it. Linger with it. Make this a daily habit.

(14) If you are going through this in a group: first, share the insights you are gleaning with one another. Second, take time to listen for one another. What do you hear the Spirit saying to you for each other?

Notes

Notes

Four

REPENTANCE

Preparation work for this chapter:

Read *Soul Care* Principle #2: Repentance

In the Soul Care video series, watch the video on repentance

In the Soul Care eCourse, watch lessons 11-15

Summary of Soul Care Principle #2: Repentance

We always have to remember that the biblical message of repentance is part of the Good News of the gospel of Christ. Both Jesus and John the Baptist proclaimed the good news of the Kingdom of God, and both began with, "Repent." In Jesus' mind, therefore, repentance is good news. Sadly, too often in the church, when we think about repentance we think about a weighty, heavy message that makes us feel bad. The ultimate goal of repentance, though, isn't to make us feel bad, but to get us aligned properly with God so we can experience freedom.

In Acts chapter 3, Peter and John lead a man to be healed in Jesus' name. A crowd gathers as this lame man runs through the temple, and Peter preaches the good news to the crowd. He calls his listeners to repent and, in Acts 3:19, the apostle says, "Repent, then, and turn to God, so that your sins may be wiped out, that times of refreshing may come from the Lord." See, that is why repentance is good news. It wipes away our sin.

When we have unconfessed sin we carry the weight of sin, guilt, shame, and condemnation, but when we repent, our sins are wiped away. That's good news! And Peter says, "Times of refreshing may come from the Lord." Jesus compared the Holy Spirit to a river (John 7:37). He picked up this image from Ezekiel 47, where the River of God flows from the temple, and everything that touches the river lives. It is the River of Life, the River of God's presence. When we dwell in the River of God's presence, we experience abundant life. But when we get out of step with the Spirit, when we sin, we step out of the River of God, and we wander into a desolate wasteland, where it is arid and nearly lifeless. Repentance is an invitation to get back into the River of God, where everything lives, and where times of refreshing come from the Lord. This is why repentance is good news!

Repentance is a critically important concept in the Kingdom of God. "There is no entrance into the kingdom without repentance. There is no advancement in the kingdom without repentance" (*Soul Care*, 2016, p. 74). In today's world, the measure for morality, most often, is what feels right to a person. But we live in a world with laws. We have laws of nature; for example, the law of gravity. You can choose to ignore it, but if you jump off a twenty-story building, I guarantee you will fall. Denying the law doesn't make it less real; you can choose to jump, but you cannot choose the consequences when you jump. In the same way, there are inviolable laws of the soul, just as with the laws of nature. You can self-define morality in any way you want, but you cannot violate the laws of the soul without consequences. For example, you have to forgive people when they hurt you. If you don't, there will be consequences for the embittered soul. You can choose bitterness, but you cannot choose the consequences of being bitter. Repentance calls us back to God's ways, brings us back into alignment with God, and allows us to experience our sins being wiped away and times of refreshing to come from the Lord. "It is soul-refreshing to be in right alignment with God" (*Soul Care*, 2016, p. 75).

The greatest enemy to repentance is pride. We must fight our base instinct to resist the Holy Spirit. The Holy Spirit never shines light into our hearts to make us feel bad; the Holy Spirit shines light to get us free. Light is a gift; it is not an intruder. We need to welcome the light God offers.

The Holy Spirit never shines light into our hearts to make us feel bad; the Holy Spirit shines light to get us free. Light is a gift; it is not an intruder.

The Apostle John wrote, "This is the message we have heard from him and declare to you: God is light; in him there is no darkness at all. If we claim to have fellowship with him and yet walk in the darkness, we lie and do not live out the truth. But if we walk in the light, as he is in the light, we have fellowship with one another, and the blood of Jesus, his Son, purifies us from all sin" (1 John 1:5-7, TNIV).

If you notice, John makes a leap of logic. He says that God is light, and that in Him there is no darkness. Then he says that if we walk in the light as He is in the light, we will have fellowship with one another. We would have expected John to say that we have fellowship with Him, but he doesn't; he says we will have fellowship "with one another." Here is John's logic: the apostle assumes that if I am really in the light with God, I will be in the light with my friend or my wife. If I am not in the light with Jen, it is because I am pretending to be better with her than I really am, and if I am pretending to be better than I am, that is pride. If I am proud with Jen, I am not in the light with God at all, because God opposes the proud. He does, though, give grace to the humble.

When I understood this truth, I determined to live without secrets, but to live instead in the light with God and others. As I began to live in the light with God and others—a life without secrets—I discovered the power and freedom of living in the light. This repentance broke shame and condemnation's grip upon me and helped me live in victory.

We have to develop a humble and contrite heart before the Lord. We must choose to respond to the Lord's correction with humility. The first thing God does to correct us is He convicts us. "Sin threatens to harden our hearts and get us out of the river of God's presence. Conviction is designed to soften our hearts and bring us back into the river, so He pricks our conscience" (*Soul Care*, 2016, p.79). We must respond to the conviction of the Spirit, bow our stiff necks, and say "yes" to God. When the Holy Spirit convicts you, it is always for specific, unconfessed sin. The Holy Spirit doesn't convict you of things you have already repented of, and the Holy Spirit is not generic. The enemy's condemnation is often generic and about already confessed sin. The enemy says, "You are a lousy Christian." That could even be true, but it is not the conviction of the Holy Spirit—it is condemnation. When the Holy Spirit convicts, there is always a specific path forward. You can take responsibility, repent, and find your sin wiped away and times of refreshing from the Lord: "You said that unkind word to your neighbor. Apologize." You own your part, humble yourself before God and your neighbor, and you can rectify it and get back into the river where everything lives.

Authentic humility begins with honesty, ends with responsibility, and somewhere in the middle is death to self, where we stop making it too much about us; instead, we make it about Jesus and others. That's the path forward that leads to the River of Life.

If we ignore the conviction of the Spirit, the Lord doesn't give up on us. He tries to get us to turn back to Him through the law of the harvest. Galatians 6:7, 8: "Do not be deceived: God cannot be mocked. People reap what they sow. Those who sow to please their sinful nature, from that nature will reap destruction." God allows the consequences of our choices to take effect in our lives to get us to repent. The conviction of the Spirit, and the law of the harvest, are not punitive in nature; they are restorative. God is trying to get us out of the desolate wasteland and back into the River of Life!

If we still do not respond to conviction and the law of the harvest, God uses discipline to correct us and return us to Himself. Discipline is not a consequence, but the hand of God seeking to bring correction. Scripture makes it clear that all God's children are disciplined, and that once again, discipline is not punitive but restorative (Hebrews 12:7-11). It is designed to produce holiness in us so that we experience the freedom, fullness, and abundant life God desires for us.

When God seeks to correct us, our job is to humble ourselves. We must live in the light with God and others and take responsibility for our lives. "The beautiful message of the Gospel is that though you are deeply flawed, you are even more deeply loved" (*Soul Care,* 2016, p. 83). "God cannot cleanse our excuses. God cannot pardon our denials. God cannot cleanse that which we will not confess. God cannot heal that which we will not admit. There is no freedom without forgiveness, and there is no forgiveness without repentance. Hiding creates darkness, and darkness destroys the soul" *(Soul Care,* p. 83). This is why repentance is good news—it gets us out of the darkness, out of the desolate wasteland of sin, and back into the River of God where our sins are wiped away and times of refreshing can come from the Lord.

God has more grace than we have sin. The only thing that prevents us from experiencing God's grace is our pride. We simply need to humble ourselves and fight our base instinct to resist the Holy Spirit. This is why I committed to live in the light with God and others.

God has more grace than we have sin. The only thing that prevents us from experiencing God's grace is our pride.

Sometimes we get stuck in the desolate wasteland of the wilderness because we confess our sins with worldly sorrow instead of godly sorrow. Paul talks about the difference in 2 Corinthians 7: "Godly sorrow brings repentance that leads to salvation and leaves no regret, but worldly sorrow brings death." Paul is writing to believers, so he is not telling them to repent of their sins and put their faith in Jesus so they can be forgiven and saved. They have already done that. He is talking about living in the fullness of salvation. He is saying that sometimes we confess our sin with worldly sorrow, but this "confession" doesn't lead us back to the River of Life. What is the difference between worldly sorrow and godly sorrow? Worldly sorrow is self-focused: "I am sorry I got caught. I am sorry you're upset with me. I am sorry this has hurt my reputation and that there are consequences for my actions." But true godly sorrow is focused outwardly, not on the inward. We are focused on God and others: "I am sorry my sin has grieved you, Lord, and I am sorry my sin has hurt others." True godly sorrow leads us back to the river, back to alignment with God, and back to the fullness of our salvation. Godly sorrow flows from a broken and contrite heart.

Here are a few things we can do to cultivate godly sorrow: (1) *Ask God for a humble, contrite heart.* Ezekiel 36:26: "I will give you a new heart and put a new spirit in you; I will remove from you your heart of stone and give you a heart of flesh." Whenever I sense my heart hardening, when I am resistant to owning my part, when I am defensive rather than contrite, I call out to God to remove my heart of stone. (2) To cultivate godly sorrow, *stand in the light with God and others.* When we blame, excuse, justify, rationalize, and deny our sin, it always hardens our heart. Stand in the light with God and others. Humble yourself before the Lord. (3) To cultivate godly sorrow, *take full ownership for your part.* If you are in a relational conflict and that conflict is 80 percent the other person's fault and 20 percent your fault, all God wants from you is to own 100 percent of your 20 percent. Here is the hard part: own your part even if the other person owns 0 percent of their 80 percent! That is between them and God. Just own your part. You are the only one responsible for you.

Sometimes we get stuck in the wasteland of the desert because of shame. We confess our sin, but we don't feel forgiven. When you confess the same thing multiple times, it is because of shame. We know the truth: we know that when we confess our sins we are forgiven (1 John 1:9). But we need revelation from the Holy Spirit to release us from our guilt, condemnation, and shame. Satan always wants me to keep my religious life private. But privatized religion produces shame that leaves me in bondage. John calls us to live in the light with God and others because it breaks the grip of shame. Humbling myself and being honest often breaks me free from shame and frees me from the enemy's grip.

Romans 8:1: "Therefore, there is now no condemnation for those who are in Christ Jesus." I do not believe that is merely a positional truth; it is a reality that God wants us to live with each day of our lives. He wants us to repent and have our sins wiped away, just as Peter said. So if shame impacts you, go to Jesus and wait on Him for revelation of these truths that you know in your Bible. Ask Jesus to illuminate these Scriptural truths to your heart and soul, that the shame will be broken and the condemnation lifted. And then, humble yourself, confess to another brother or sister, and live in the light with God and others. There is freedom in Christ—not just when you get to Heaven, but here and now.

Remember: unconfessed sin can reap havoc in our lives. David said, "When I kept silent, my bones wasted away through my groaning all day long. For day and night your hand was heavy on me; my strength was sapped as in the heat of summer" (Psalm 32:3, 4). David's sin was weighing on him—physically, emotionally, spiritually. I cannot tell you how many times through the years someone came to me with an ailment (physical or emotional) and wanted prayer. When I went to pray, I heard the Lord say, "They have a secret," or, "Bitterness"—something to that effect. I told the person what I heard, and then they confessed their sin, and Jesus not only broke their shame, He also released them from the havoc it was reaping in their lives. Be honest. Walk in the light. There is freedom there; light always dispels darkness.

Be honest. Walk in the light. There is freedom there; light always dispels darkness.

I have chosen to die with no secrets. I have a few people in my life that know everything about me; I have done a "total life confession" with my friends Martin, Ron, Rich, and my wife Jen. No one can come to me today and say "you did such and such" except that I can say, "Yes, but Martin knew that; Ron knows that; Rich knows that. Jen knows that. Heck, I wrote that one in a book." The power of living like this is that Satan cannot hold my past over me. I have brought it all into the light, and shame has been broken. If you have never done a total life confession, I encourage you to do so.

Experiences

(1) Make it a habit every day to update your confessions. Ask the Lord: "Search me, God, and know my heart; test me and know my anxious thoughts. See if there is any offensive way in me, and lead me in the way everlasting" (Psalm 139:23, 24). Take time right now. Make sure your confessions are up to date. Linger with God; let Him bring up anything you need to confess. When necessary, apologize to anyone that you have hurt or sinned against. Include this in your daily prayer time—either in the evening or in the morning. Take time to ask the Lord to search you, and then confess your sins. God never shines light to make you feel bad; He shines light to set you free.

(2) "The enemy of our souls makes honesty terrifying and secrets appealing, but only as we walk in the light with God and others can we truly get free" (*Soul Care*, 2016, p. 85). Why is being honest with others about our sin something to fear? What makes keeping our sin secret so appealing? Even though it is scary, why does God invite us to bring our sin into the light? Have you had times where you have been honest with someone about wrongdoing and experienced a release from guilt, shame, and condemnation?

(3) When the Holy Spirit convicts us, it is always about specific, unconfessed sin. But the enemy condemns us over sins we have already confessed, and he condemns us with generic attacks (e.g, "you're a lousy person" or "you are always fearful"). Where have you been living under condemnation in your life? What past issues is the enemy bringing to your attention and haunting you with? Have you been honest and confessed those to a safe, gracious person? Where does the enemy attack you with generic condemnations?

(4) We have to fight our base instinct to resist the Holy Spirit. Are there any areas where you have been resisting the conviction of the Holy Spirit? Are there any particular areas where the Holy Spirit has been calling you to be honest and you have resisted? Where have you been living under the consequences of your sin? How can you humble yourself and take responsibility for your part? The Lord doesn't allow consequences to punish us but to restore us. What is the Lord showing you, teaching you, and calling you to take responsibility for?

(5) Are there any areas in your life where you have confessed sin but don't feel forgiven? Where is shame impacting you? How do you describe the presence of shame on your soul? What does it feel like? What sins have you confessed more than once—even though you may have only committed the sin once, or you left it behind a while back. You did that sin long ago, perhaps, or you have broken free from it, but it still haunts you, and the enemy still brings it up and condemns you. Bring that to the Lord right now. Picture Him standing in front of you. Hand Him that sin. Call it what it is; don't spin it. Wait on the Lord for release. What is the Lord showing you, saying to you? Jesus doesn't want you to simply know you are forgiven and then continue living under condemnation. He wants you to live free from the enemy's guilt, shame, and condemnation.

6) Is the Lord inviting you to humbly confess your sins to another? Privatized religion produces shame that leaves us in bondage. Who do you need to walk in the light with? What haunts you that you need to bring into the light with a safe brother or sister?

(7) Are there any patterns of sin in your life that are characterized by worldly sorrow not godly sorrow? Worldly sorrow is focused on self, not on God and others. What is God calling you to do about that? What does God want you to do so you can break free from worldly sorrow?

(8) Are you willing to do a total life confession with another person? Who would you do that with? Perhaps you have been working through this with a group, and you want to do it together. If you don't have anyone yet, then work toward building those kinds of true friendships. Find someone to open up with. Share something that is honest and vulnerable but won't destroy you if the person possibly would betray you. Then, if they are honorable and gracious with that confession, open up some more. If they continue to be honorable and gracious, invite them to work with you through Soul Care and do a life confession with you. When you are finished, be sure to have no skeletons left in your closet—leave no haunting, untold secrets.

(9) Meditate on Romans 8:1: "Therefore, there is no condemnation for those who are in Christ Jesus." Let the Holy Spirit personalize that truth to you over any and all sins that have left you feeling shamed and condemned. What do you sense the Lord saying to you?

(10) Do you have anyone you need to apologize to? It is possible that you are in a relational conflict where it is 20 percent your fault and 80 percent the other person's fault. All God wants from you is to own 100 percent of your 20 percent. Owning our part does not validate what the other person has done. It simply is an act of humility before God, and God honors the humble. Make it a habit in your life to regularly confess and ask forgiveness of anyone you sin against.

(11) I know my heart is growing hard when I am reluctant to own my part, when I am quick to blame and slow to take responsibility for my part. I know my heart is growing hard when I'm resistant to the Holy Spirit's prompting to apologize and confess to another. What are some of the symptoms of pride in your life? Do you see any place where pride is lurking? What is the Lord calling you to do?

(12) You may want to walk through Neil Anderson's *Steps to Freedom*. It is an excellent tool to help people make sure their confessions are current and/or to do a total life confession.

Notes

Notes

Five

OVERCOMING FAMILY SIN PATTERNS

Preparation work for this chapter:

Read *Soul Care* Principle #3: Overcoming Family Sin Patterns

In the Soul Care video series, watch: Overcoming Family Sin Patterns

In the Soul Care eCourse, watch lessons 16-19

Summary of Soul Care Principle #3: Overcoming Family Sin Patterns

The Bible says that the sins of the parents visit their children. We see this reality in our own lives and in the lives of Bible characters. Think about David. David commits adultery with a woman named Bathsheba, who was a longtime family friend (her husband, Uriah, was one of David's mighty men; they had battled and traveled together for many years). He then has her husband, Uriah, intentionally killed in a battle. So he commits sins of sexual immorality and violence, but we especially want to notice how these sin patterns then impact his children.

His son Amnon rapes his daughter Tamar—sex and violence are now combined in one act. The sex between David and Bathsheba was consensual, but Amnon's was rape, and it was incestuous. Later, Absalom tries to kill his father and take over David's kingdom; he also sleeps with his father's concubines in public—once again we see the pattern of sexual immorality and violence. Then there is Solomon. Solomon has one thousand wives . . . which would be excessive by any standard! He has an insatiable appetite and never says no to himself. Many of the women he marries are foreigners, who worship other deities, and sadly, Solomon ends up worshiping demonic entities. God sends him an adversary to correct his rebellious path, but rather than humbling himself and repenting,

Solomon attempts to kill the one God sent him for correction. Once again, sex and violence impact the family.

This is why we have to deal with family sin patterns. If not, they will impact our children and our children's children.

Think about Abraham. One of the sins Abraham commits is lying (though I would argue it is not his worst sin), and the real motive for his lying is undealt-with fear. But let's look at lying. He tells the lie that his wife is not his sister because he is afraid other people are going to try to steal his wife. His son Isaac repeats the same lie. He can't even make up his own lie; he has to steal his old man's lie! And the next generation, Jacob, is called "the deceiver." We can see this is not headed in a good direction!

I would argue that Abraham's worst sin, however, is favoritism. Abraham and Sarah favor Isaac—to the point that they kick Abraham's son Ishmael out of the house and are willing to let him die in the wilderness! This is a vile, wicked deed. The next generation, Isaac, has a favorite; his favorite is Esau. But this time his wife, Rebecca, has a different favorite, Jacob. The result is division, manipulation, and control that destroys the family. Then we follow Jacob's story, and Jacob too has a favorite—Joseph, whom he dresses up in a fancy coat and parades in front of his brothers. The explicit favoritism does not go over well, and the brothers have a council to decide whether they should kill Joseph or sell him into slavery. Do you feel the weightiness of family sin patterns? This is why we must address them.

"Family sin patterns have unusual pull on our souls; they are often the most stubborn sin patterns to break" (*Soul Care,* 2016, p. 100). I think they are more difficult to break because they are modeled for us—thus, they become normal to us. Plus, as they are passed from generation to generation, they often gain demonic strength. And finally, I think there is something to be said for DNA. David says that he was sinful in his mother's womb. He hadn't chosen sin yet, but a sinful nature is inherited from fallen parents, and we have a natural tendency to sin in the direction of our ancestors. This is part of the sinful nature.

The most honorable thing we can ever do for our family name is to break free from these patterns of behavior. I never wanted to explore my family sin patterns to blame my family, but for the simple reason that I wanted to get free and honor God and my family. There is no honor if we simply repeat the dishonorable things our family has done. This is why we need to explore these areas—so we can develop self-awareness and, ultimately, freedom.

Sometimes we try to gain freedom by rebelling against our family sin patterns. But there is no freedom in rebellion. You are a spiritual being in a spiritual world; you are always giving away spiritual access. You don't get to choose *if* you give away spiritual access; you only get to choose *to whom* you give away spiritual access. If you pick up the tools of the enemy, you are giving access to the evil one. Rebellion is a tool of the enemy. Jesus never rebels. He only did what the Father told Him to do, only went where the Father told Him to go, and only said what the Father told Him to say. Jesus lived in perfect submission to the Father. In the spiritual kingdom there is no freedom through rebellion; it comes only in submission to the King. We have to bring these patterns into the light with God and learn how to submit to Jesus in order to find freedom.

So how do we find the victory Jesus has provided?

> We have to bring these patterns into the light with God, and we have to be ruthlessly honest about our families and with ourselves.

First, if we are going to get free, *we have to begin with self-awareness.* Self-awareness is the gateway to transformation; it doesn't guarantee transformation and freeness, but you can't get there without it. You cannot heal that which you will not admit. We have to bring these patterns into the light with God, and we have to be ruthlessly honest about our families and with ourselves. For some of us, it is more difficult to be honest about our families. We can see our flaws, but we tend to idealize our families. I sometimes listen to people's stories, and I hear the stuff they are wrestling with, the dysfunction that plagues them, yet when I ask them to tell me about their family, they tell me a nearly idyllic tale. The problem is the story doesn't add up; they didn't get this way, with all these problems, from that beginning point. They aren't being honest about their family, and they need to be honest if they are going to get free.

For others, it is more difficult to be honest about themselves. For example, in my own case, I could see that my dad was angry when I grew up. His anger was more roaring; he had a short fuse. The way I processed this was that I did not want to be angry; in fact, in my mind, anger was evil. So I couldn't be angry. When Jen and I got married, she would say to me, "Are you angry with me?" I would say, "No, I'm not angry, I'm just upset" (or "disappointed," or some other euphemism). Eventually, with God's help, I came to realize that I was in fact angry, but my anger wasn't like my dad's. I didn't yell, it wasn't roaring; it was more like a frozen lake. I would create a wall of silence when I was angry with Jen, but she still felt the anger. She felt like she was walking on eggshells around me because I was radiating anger even if I wasn't communicating it. I had to get honest with myself and admit that I, too, was an angry man; my anger was just expressed differently. That was the first key to gaining victory.

Second, if we are to gain freedom from our family sin patterns, *we need to be careful not to compromise in these areas.* Be sure to stay in the light with God and others. Family sin patterns are like a riptide—if you are not careful, they will pull you out to sea. Often, we need help in these areas, but because we have been sworn to secrecy in our family, or because these areas are so packed with shame, we don't seek the help we need to overcome. Humble yourself and reach out for the help you need.

There are two types of people to reach out to: (1) Reach out to a wise spiritual guide who can pray with you and help you navigate these turbulent, troubling areas. This could be a wise friend, a counselor, a spiritual director, or a pastor. Whoever you wisely choose, reach out to someone you are committed to being honest with, and radically repent and have them pray with you through these areas. In my case, I reached out to my friend Martin Sanders. Martin was ten and half years older than me. I shared with him the pattern of sexual immorality in my family, and I told him I was afraid I would follow my family into this sin. Martin said to me, "You will finish as a man of God, and I will walk with you all your days." Jen is still the only woman I have ever been with, and I am living victoriously. Martin and I continued to walk with one another in the light until Martin died in January 2024. I am grateful I reached out for help. (2) Develop some gracious prayer partners with whom you have a no-pretending policy. In the early days, I reached out to my friend Rich Schmidt and, if I was feeling tempted to lust, would write him an email and say, "Pray for me." Then on Fridays, in a regularly scheduled phone call, we updated our confessions. It was a vital link to victory. In the later days, Martin became my closest friend and gracious prayer partner, and we regularly confessed our sins with one another and reached out to each other for help and prayer support.

Third, if you want to live in freedom over your family sins, *deal severely with sin before it deals severely with you.* Jesus said, "You have heard that it was said, 'Do not commit adultery.' But I tell you that anyone who looks at a woman lustfully has already committed adultery with her in his heart. If your right eyes causes you to sin, gouge it out and throw it away. It is better for you to lose one part of your body than for you whole body to be thrown into hell" (Matthew 5:27-29). Jesus is urging us to deal radically with sin before sin deals radically with us. So, for example, in my own battle to get free from the lust that had impacted my family, Jen and I decided to get rid of our TV for a season. I knew that if we had a TV, sometimes the images would cause me to lust, so it was better if I didn't have one. I took a severe step to break free from the temptation to lust. At this point in our lives, we have a TV, but I never turn it on because I don't know how to! I have to call my son to help me turn it on if I want to watch anything! I stay in hotels more than one hundred nights a year, but I never turn on the TV. Here is the point: it no longer has a pull on me because I dealt severely with the family sin pattern.

Fourth, if you want to get free from family sin patterns, *practice spiritual disciplines that counteract your family sin.* Certain disciplines counteract certain sins more effectively. Let me use addiction as an example. All addictions have three things in common: (1) They are rooted in shame. We feel bad inside—feelings like "I am not lovable," "something is wrong with me," "I don't have what it takes"—so we turn to alcohol, for example, to numb the negative feelings. And it works, but only for a little while, and then the feelings come back, so we pick up the bottle again—and again, and again. Soon we become addicted, as it takes more to satisfy less. (2) All addicts are liars. It is the nature of shame and addiction. We sneak out to the garage to drink, and our spouse confronts us: "Have you been drinking?" And we lie. "No, I haven't been drinking." We do this because we feel ashamed. We have the primary shame that drove us to drink, and now we have a secondary shame because we are drinking too much; it is like compound interest on our shame. We fear that "if you knew me, you wouldn't love me or accept me," so we lie and feel bad because we lied. (3) All addicts are increasingly self-centered. We keep feeding our self-life. The more we engage in addictive behavior, the more we feed our self-life, and the more addicted to self we become. When I was a pastor and dealing with addicts, I would always encourage the person, if they wanted to get free, to go on a two-week fast. Why? Well, there is power in fasting, but more than that, fasting is an act of self-denial. It is breaking the pattern to feed your self-life. Then I would have that person do a life confession, and this works to call them to break the pattern of lying and get completely honest with someone who will love them as they are. And then I helped them deal with the roots of shame. Fasting and the discipline of honesty as a lifestyle become vital to helping people who struggle with addiction to break free.

Finally, if you want to find freedom from a family sin pattern, *mediate on Scriptures that focus on the virtue you want to construct in your life.* "Meditation moves truth from your head to your heart. It embeds the truth of God's Word into your heart as a core value, and out of the overflow of the heart we speak and act (Matthew 12:34; Matthew 15:18, 19; Luke 6:45)" (*Soul Care,* 2016, p. 115). In my early years in marriage, I realized I was wrestling with selfishness. So I started meditating on Philippians 2:3, 4: "Do nothing out of selfish ambition or vain conceit, but in humility consider others better than yourselves. Each of you should look not only to your own interest, but also to the interest of others." I would meditate on this for a little while and pray it into my life at breakfast, lunch, dinner, and bedtime. Believe it or not, the first thing I noticed was that I was becoming a more considerate driver! I was letting people out in front of me (somewhat like I was the mayor in town and needed their vote!). After a little while Jen came to me and said, "What's with you? You're helpful." I said, "I'm always helpful." She said, "No. You're not. Seriously, what happened?" I told her I realized I was selfish, so I started meditating on this passage to help break that pattern. She said, "It's working. You need to keep it up." (I said, "I have a few I'd like you to meditate on, if you want to go there!")

There is no soul in bondage beyond God's redemptive reach; there is no sin damage beyond God's reparative presence.

"No matter how dark your family dysfunction, no matter how strong the riptide of your sin patterns, God can set you free. There is no soul in bondage beyond God's redemptive reach; there is no sin damage beyond God's reparative presence" (*Soul Care,* 2016, p. 120).

Experiences

(1) **Take time to reflect and journal on your own family. What are some of the sin patterns you see? If you think there are none, you aren't being honest. How have those patterns impacted you? (Remember, it may look different in you than it did in your mom or dad.) We never look at our family sins to blame our families; we do so to get free so we can more fully honor God and our families. Do you tend to idealize your family or blame your family? Which are you more likely to do?**

(2) **"Sometimes we see our family sin and we rebel against it in an effort to overcome it. But there is no victory in rebellion, only in submission to the King . . . rebellion only leads to different forms of bondage" (*Soul Care*, 2016, p. 104). (Example: Grandpa was an alcoholic. Dad never drinks, but he became a fundamentalist; he opts for the strong control of legalism to make him feel safe after growing up in a home out of control. But he never dealt with the roots of shame, and his son ends up going back to a lifestyle of addiction.) Are there any areas where you have used rebellion against a family sin? Or in which you see that happening in your family?**

(3) Do you need to talk to your family about your family history? What questions do you need to ask? Who do you need to talk to in the family? Who is keeper of the secrets? Make sure your approach is honorable. We never want to blame our family. I went and talked to my grandmother. In my family it was not normal to talk about sex, but I went and talked to my grandmother about sex because I wanted to get free. This was the approach I used with my grandparents: "Gram and Pop, I love you, and I love Jesus. I want to honor our family and honor Jesus, but I am struggling with lust. I haven't been with anyone but Jen, I am not looking at pornography, but I am struggling with lustful thoughts. I know there are some stories about people with sexual immorality in our family—some public examples of sexual sin—but I sense that this is just the tip of the iceberg. I feel like I am fighting a battle with one hand tied behind my back, and I'm asking you to tell me the family story so I can get free and honor Jesus and the family." These conversations aren't easy to have but can be vital to victory. My grandparents shared the history with me, and it has helped me on my journey to freedom. If you find people willing to talk to you, ask questions about the history of the family, about the family patterns. Ask questions about the patterns you have struggled with personally. Ask questions about family secrets.

(4) There are only two ways to find out knowledge about your family history: natural knowledge and supernatural knowledge. You have to have the conversations that no one likes to have and gain as much natural knowledge as you can. But if your family is all gone, or they won't talk to you, or you have been adopted and you don't know any of them or your story, then you have to discover what you need to know through supernatural knowledge. The Lord will reveal what you need to know. He won't tell you things to satisfy your curiosity,

but He will show you what you need to know to get free. If you need supernatural knowledge, set aside a day to pray and fast and wait on the Lord. You might need to do this multiple times over the next year. Daily, ask the Lord to reveal things that you need to know. You may have images, dreams, or words that reveal things to you. You may also consider getting some discerning person to help you pray, fast, and listen.

(5) Examine your life. Where do you have vulnerabilities to your family sins that need more protective measures? Where are you compromising, getting too close to the edge, and find that you need to take a step back? How can you set up a few safety fences that will ultimately produce more freedom in your life?

(6) Who do you have in your life right now that you are completely honest with? Do you need to develop a friend with whom you have a non-pretending policy? Do you need a wise spiritual guide in some area to help you navigate to freedom? Who could you reach out to for help?

(7) What family sin patterns do you need to deal severely with? What would it look like to deal severely with that sin pattern to help find victory? Ask the Lord for insight on what steps to take. Talk to your gracious prayer partners or spiritual guides to help find a path forward.

(8) What spiritual disciplines could help you overcome your family sin patterns? Ask the Holy Spirit for wisdom. Spend time waiting on God and listening. Again, seek out spiritual counselors and friends for insights.

(9) What virtues do you need to build into your life? What Scriptures can you meditate on to help?

(10) You may want to create a Genogram. Just google Genogram and you will find free websites that can help you create one. A genogram is a family tree that helps you see patterns; things are visibly laid out before you. It can be an effective tool. It can be helpful to do this with a group of people you are working with as you go through Soul Care. Share your Genograms with each other.

(11) If you are stuck in a family sin pattern, set aside a day to meet alone with God. Fast and pray on your retreat day. Ask the Lord to show you the roots to the behavior pattern in your life and in the life of your family. I would encourage you to get a copy of the book *The Soul Care Leader* and read chapters 6 and 7, "Taking Versus Processing" and "Digging Up the Roots." These chapters will help you gain freedom. Process the chapters slowly, reflectively, prayerfully with God.

(12) As you seek to gain freedom, you may want to fast one day a week with a prayer partner. Be sure to meditate on the Scriptures that have the virtues you want to construct. Also, this is a good time to update your confessions with your prayer partner.

Notes

Notes

Six

FORGIVENESS

Preparation work for this chapter:

Read *Soul Care* Principle #4: Forgiveness

In the video series, watch: Forgiveness

In the Soul Care eCourse, watch lessons 20-23

Summary of Soul Care Principle #4: Forgiveness

We need to forgive those who sin against us, or we will never walk in freedom and fullness in Christ. This is the very nature of God: to forgive. In Ephesians 4:26, 27, Paul writes, "'In your anger do not sin.' Do not let the sun go down while you are still angry, and do not give the devil a foothold." I don't think Paul means that, literally, we should never let the sun go down while we are angry; he is simply using a metaphor to tell us we need to deal with our anger quickly. Do not let it accumulate in your soul. It is not a sin to be angry, but when we are angry, we are more likely to sin, so we must deal with it quickly. If we don't deal with it, the enemy can gain access to us through our anger. Remember what we have said earlier: we are spiritual beings in a spiritual world; we are always giving away spiritual access. We don't get to choose *if* we give away access; we only get to choose *to whom* we give away access. If we pick up the tools of the enemy, we are giving access to the evil one. So rather than holding on to our anger and giving the enemy our access, we need to give God access and forgive.

That's why Paul, in this context, goes on to say, "Be kind and compassionate to one another, forgiving each other, just as in Christ God forgave you" (Ephesians 4:32). We need to choose obedience and process our anger and hurt and forgive those who sin against us.

"Forgiveness is a matter of obedience, not a matter of more faith. Forgiveness is your responsibility and choice, not God's responsibility. Forgiveness is the duty of a faithful follower made possible by the grace he or she has received. You have to choose to forgive. You have to resolve to release people from your debt" (*Soul Care*, 2016, p. 127).

Why Should We Forgive?

First, *we ought to forgive because we have been forgiven.* This is the single most-often noted, most important motivation for forgiving others in the Bible. In Matthew 18, Jesus tells the parable of the unmerciful servant. It is a story of a man who owes a ludicrous amount of money to his master. The man can never pay it back, and by the custom of the day he was to be sold into slavery along with his family. The man pleads for time and, he says, he will pay back the debt. The master took pity on him and canceled the debt. If the story ended there, it would be a story of beautiful magnanimity. Sadly, the story doesn't end there. The man goes out and finds a fellow servant who owes him one hundred days' worth of wages. This amount is not an insignificant amount of money, but it is a repayable sum. The fellow servant begs the first man for time to pay it back, just as the first man had asked for, but this unmerciful servant refuses. When the master finds out, he is angry and holds the servant to account. Jesus' point is simple: it is utterly ludicrous for us to hold someone in our debt given how much the Lord has forgiven us over our lifetime. We forgive because we have been forgiven. And the only reason we don't forgive is because we do not realize how much we have been forgiven.

The only reason we don't forgive is because we do not realize how much we have been forgiven.

Second, *we should forgive because bitterness gives Satan a foothold; it gives him access to our souls.* When we hold a grudge, the enemy torments us. Anger is like a shield that we use to protect ourselves. The problem with shields is they are indiscriminate. They not only block out the person we perceive is trying to hurt us, they also block God from trying to heal us. The only one who gets access behind the shield is the enemy, who handed the thing to us in the first place. We have this wound in our soul because we have been hurt, and the enemy sees we are longing for some comfort, so he offers us a comfort sin pattern—drinking, or lust, or something of this sort to make us feel better. We pick up this comfort sin to take the edge off our pain, and then he grabs it like a club and beats us with it: "You call yourself a Christian, and look at what you did!" He condemns us, and we are handed over to the torturers (as Jesus says in the parable of the unmerciful servant). The only way out of the torment is to give God access and forgive.

Third, *we should forgive because bitterness is corrosive.* It is like poison; we end up hurting ourselves with our anger. But it is also corrosive to the family of God. Hebrews 12:15 says, "See to it that no one falls short of the grace of God and that no bitter root grows up to cause trouble and defile many." When we are angry, we end up spilling negativity and judgment toward those who hurt us. Often, we share these things with others and sour their opinion on the people who hurt us.

How Do You Forgive?

First, if we want to forgive those who sin against us, *we begin by soaking in the grace of God.* This is where the unmerciful servant takes a wrong turn. Imagine you had a $500,000 mortgage and someone wrote it off for you. Wouldn't you take time to celebrate? I would run home doing an Irish jig! But this guy never celebrates; he never soaks in the elaborate grace he received. If we rehearse our hurt, rather than celebrate God's grace, we will be left to the torturers. So sing songs about God's grace; meditate on Scriptures about God's grace; recall all the things God has forgiven us for and take time to celebrate the grace of God. It will help soften our heart.

But this guy never celebrates; he never soaks in the elaborate grace he received. If we rehearse our hurt, rather than celebrate God's grace, we will be left to the torturers.

Second, *bless those who curse you.* Pray all the good things you want in your life for those who have hurt you. Jesus said, "Love your enemies, do good to those who hate you, bless those who curse you, pray for those who mistreat you" (Luke 6:27, 28). The Lord taught me early in my ministry to bless those who curse, and it has made a huge difference in my life. It has become my reflex reaction when someone does something to hurt me. I pray blessings on the person. I don't feel like it; I do it because Jesus told me to, and I trust Him and love Him. I have discovered that if you do what God tells you to do, God will do what you cannot do: He will change your heart.

Third, *if we are going to forgive those who sin against us, it helps to see ourselves more like than unlike our offender.* We tend to villainize the people who hurt us; we see them as only evil all the time, and we begin to judge their motives through that negative lens. But it helps to understand their story and have some compassion for why they do what they do. It doesn't give them excuses, but it does give us sympathy, and that helps us soften our hearts and forgive.

Fourth, *offer forgiveness to the level of the offense.* Let's say we were talking today and I said something that hurt you. You came to me and told me that I had hurt you, and I apologize: "I'm sorry. Please forgive me." You say you forgive me, but tomorrow you come back and say, "When you said that to me yesterday, that really hurt me." I protest: "But we talked about it yesterday, and I asked you to forgive me, and you forgave me." You acknowledged that to be true, so I ask, "Why are we still talking about it?" Most often the answer is because what I said was a 5-gallon offense, but we only exchanged a cup worth of apology and forgiveness; there are still 4.8 gallons left in the tank. This is why, so often, people keep cycling through the same conversations with some people—we have to forgive to the level of the offense. Now, often, the deeper problem is with families, because sometimes there isn't a mere five gallons of offense but a whole pond full of hurt that needs to be processed and forgiven.

Fifth, *we have to choose forgiveness.* "Forgiveness is a gift offered by the offended party. It is never deserved or earned. Therefore, you can forgive someone unilaterally; they don't need to apologize" (*Soul Care,* 2016, p.139). This is a gift from God to you; otherwise, you would always be bound by the rebellious will of another person who refused to forgive. But you can forgive someone who will not apologize; you can even forgive someone who is dead. No one can lock you to the chain of bitterness . . . except yourself.

Now, there is a difference between forgiveness and trust. Forgiveness is a gift granted by the offended party; it is never deserved or earned. Trust, however, is earned. When someone sins against us, it damages our trust in the relationship. If the person refuses to own their part and repent, trust cannot be restored. We can forgive, but our trust will be impaired, and our relational intimacy will be shallow. Trust is the bridge of intimacy, and trust is earned. For trust to be restored in a relationship, the offending parties need to own their part, apologize, and commit to change; they need to repent. While forgiveness is *unilateral,* reconciliation is *bilateral*—it takes both parties. I need to fully own my part and forgive you for your part; you need to fully own your part and forgive me for my part.

Sixth, if we are going to forgive those who sin against us, *we need to process through forgiveness.* Sometimes forgiveness comes off in layers, somewhat like peeling an onion. That is because of the 5-gallon analogy. We may have forgiven three gallons, but there are still two gallons left in the tank. "Keep affirming the decision you have made, and keep praying blessings on the person who has sinned against you. Keep working through the process of forgiveness" (*Soul Care*, 2016, p. 140).

Sometimes we have a hard time processing through forgiveness because we are not aware how deep the hurt goes. Other times, we are still in a relationship with someone who keeps hurting us. We have to learn how to establish healthy boundaries. There is a difference between a boundary and a shield. A shield is an act of self-protection, and it allows dysfunction to rule in a relationship. For example, someone yells at me and calls me names, and either I yell, scream, and call them names back, or I turn to some passive-aggressive behavior. Either way, dysfunction is determining our interaction. A boundary elevates the conversation to a higher level of functionality; we preserve the dignity and respect of both parties. With a boundary, I may say to the person, "I'm sure what you are saying to me is important, but I would ask you to reframe the conversation and speak to me without yelling and name-calling. I will treat you with dignity and respect, and I am asking you to do the same for me." This gives the other person an opportunity to function at a higher level, and it preserves dignity and respect for all.

Seventh, *remember that God is redemptive.* Romans 8:28, 29 promises us that God can take anything that comes into our lives and use it to make us more like Jesus. It is not that everything that comes into our lives is good, but God is so good that even when someone does something evil, God can redeem it and use it for good. This is incredibly hopeful. Hope is essential for empowerment. The reason we pick up the shield of anger is because anger is empowering. When we feel hurt, we feel weak and vulnerable, but anger makes us feel powerful. In order to let go of anger, it is often helpful to pick up the empowering feeling of hope. Hope empowers us so we don't feel like we are a victim to the other person or our circumstances. At the same time, though, hope leaves us feeling as though God can make something good come from the situation. That allows us to let go of our shield of anger and trust God to forgive those who sin against us.

Eighth, *if we are going to process through forgiveness, it helps to grieve.* "You need to grieve over your losses in life: loss of relationship, loss of a dream, loss of reputation, loss of opportunity, loss of innocence, loss of love, and loss of a loved one" (*Soul Care,* 2016, p. 143). Grieving is essential to forgiveness. It helps us get in touch with our pain, and then it leads us to healing in God's presence. I often use the Psalms to help me grieve; many of the Psalms are lament psalms in which the psalmists process their negative emotions, hurts, and sufferings. If we don't grieve, we will often end up with accumulated hurts and disappointments and begin to shut down emotionally. Jesus was a man of sorrows, acquainted with grief, and He understood the importance of grieving.

If I die tonight, I have no enemies. There are people who do not like me, but the feeling is not mutual.

In the end, we have to choose to forgive those who sin against us. I have decided that I will die with no enemies in my life. If I die tonight, I have no enemies. There are people who do not like me, but the feeling is not mutual. "I have decided to bless everyone who curses me. I have determined to hold no grudges, nurse no wounds, nurture no disappointments, and hang on to no resentments. I will process my anger and pain at all costs, and I will forgive my enemies" (*Soul Care,* 2016, p. 147). Commit yourself to forgive those who sin against you and to die without a single enemy. Jesus said that even the pagans love their friends; we don't get any credit for doing that. But when we love our enemies, we reflect the heart of God to all who are near (Matthew 5:43-48).

Experiences

(1) Sit quietly before the Lord and ask Him to reveal to you anyone you need to forgive. Write a list of those you need to forgive. Don't defend yourself if a name or face comes to mind. Just write it down. Don't say, "I've already forgiven this person." Maybe you have dropped four gallons, but there is another gallon left to go. Write down all the names that come to mind, and begin praying blessings on those people. Pray blessings on them every day, and work through these steps of forgiveness until you feel released.

(2) Ask the Lord, "Is there anyone I am harboring resentments or grudges toward?" Paul told us to not let the sun go down on our anger, but some of us have wounds from as far back as our childhood, and we didn't know how to forgive those who sinned against us. Ask the Lord if there is anyone you need to forgive from your past, from your family of origin, your school years, teachers, friends, relatives, neighbors. If the Lord brings any names, faces, places, or incidents to mind, bless those who curse you and forgive those who sin against

you. Often, as children, we did not have the ability to work through the process of forgiveness, and we unintentionally allowed the sun to go down on our anger. As adults, we often need to go backward and clean up these hurts and offenses so we can move forward.

(3) The point of the parable of the unmerciful servant (Matthew 18:21-35) is this: "It is utterly absurd for us to hold someone in our debt in light of the remarkable forgiveness God has offered us" (*Soul Care*, 2016, p. 131). The only reason we hold others in our debt is because we truly do not understand how much God has forgiven us. Where have you found it difficult to receive God's forgiveness? Why has it been difficult? How has your experience of receiving God's forgiveness hindered you from forgiving others? Consider the grace of God in your life; meditate on all the ways God has forgiven you. Soak in God's grace.

(4) **"There is a difference between a shield and a boundary. A shield is something I pick up to protect myself. I can pick up defensiveness, anger, withdrawal, or silence as a shield, and I can use that shield to keep the offender away from me and protect myself. It neither protects my dignity nor the dignity of the other person. But a boundary is used to preserve both my dignity and the other person's dignity" (*Soul Care*, 2016, pp. 140, 141). What shields do you use to protect yourself? When do you use those shields? Where do you need to use healthy boundaries instead? What would healthy boundaries look like? You may need help deciding how to develop healthy boundaries.**

(5) **Most of the time I do not need to go to the person I have forgiven. If I can forgive and move on with the relationship, I do. There are three times, however, when I think that we need to go to the person and initiate a conversation. First, we go when we are in a relationship with someone and there is an ongoing offense. Follow the guidelines of Matthew 18. Our goal is restoration. Second, we go when trust has been damaged in the relationship and we value the bond we have had with the other person, and we want to repair trust so we can go deeper in intimacy. It is possible that you can forgive the person and move on, but to restore trust you have to have a conversation. Again, the goal is restoration. Third, sometimes we go to the other person for their sake. Galatians 6:1 says, "If someone is caught in a sin, you who live by the Spirit should restore that person gently. But watch yourselves, or you also may be tempted." Sometimes we go to a person because an action has become a pattern of behavior**

in the person's life. We can forgive them for what they did or said to us, but they are doing this over and over (not just the time they did it to us), and it is hurting them and hurting their relationships with others. So we go for the sake of the other person. In Galatians 6, Paul goes on to say (verse 2), "Carry each other's burdens." The burden Paul is referring to, in the context, is sin. Unbroken sinful patterns are like a heavy burden; carrying that weight is like carrying around a fifty-pound rock on your back wherever they go. Doing so is wearisome. So we who are walking in the Spirit should want to help carry the load, lift the burden, and help our brothers and sisters get free. Paul warns us to watch ourselves lest we go with a self-righteous attitude, pride, bitterness, or some other impure motive. We can go acting like we aren't hurt, pretending that we are trying to help someone else, when we're really trying to hurt the one who has hurt us. Make sure your motives are pure. Work through forgiveness before you go. Again, look at the list of people you need to forgive. Do you need to go to any of them? Ask the Lord for insight.

(6) Pay close attention to your self-talk and conversations with others. Where have you been entertaining conversations in your head with someone who has hurt you rather than blessing those who have hurt you? Where have you been talking with others about those who have hurt you rather than working through the process of forgiveness? Ask God to help you change the patterns. Make it your reflex reaction to bless those who curse you.

(7) Is there anyone in your life you are avoiding because of offense? Sometimes when we are hurt we simply avoid other people. We haven't forgiven them, and we haven't processed with them; we are merely trying to avoid them to protect ourselves. Ask the Lord to show you if there is anyone you have been avoiding, and ask Him to help you work through forgiveness toward that person.

(8) Let's spend some time soaking in the grace of God. Think of a time when you tried to clean dirty dishes and the food particles had hardened to the plate. You either had to scrub extra hard to get them off, or you could draw a sink of warm, soapy water and let them soak in the soapy solution. After leaving them there for a while, of course, the food particles are much easier to work off. Soaking in God's grace softens the hardened places in our hearts. Here are some passages to meditate on, places to soak in the grace of God:

- Matthew 27:32-56 (see tips for meditation in the Experiences section of Chapter 3 on Identity)
- Matthew 18:21-35
- Matthew 7:1-5
- Matthew 9:1-8 (Mark 2:1-12)
- Matthew 9:9-13
- Matthew 26:17-30
- Matthew 26:36-46
- Mark 14:32-42
- Mark 15:21-41
- Luke 6:27-36
- Luke 6:37-42
- Luke 7:36-50
- Luke 18:9-14
- Luke 22:7-30
- Luke 23:26-49
- John 19:18-37
- Romans 3:21-31
- Romans 5:1-11
- 1 Corinthians 13:1-13
- Philippians 2:1-11
- 1 John 2:3-11
- 1 John 4:7-21

9) You may have been victimized, but you are not a victim. In Christ, we are more than conquerors, and we can overcome. Give God access to your hurts. Acknowledge to Him where you have felt powerless. Accept your responsibility to forgive, doing so with his help. Read Romans 8:28-39; meditate on this passage. Ask the Lord how He can redeem the hurts in your life; journal some of that here. Hope is empowering, and it is an essential element in letting down the shield of anger.

(10) "You have to acknowledge your pain in the presence of God so you can access his healing love" (*Soul Care,* 2016, p. 146). Take a moment to write down and reflect on any unresolved relational hurts you have experienced. Sit in Jesus' presence with those hurts, give them to Jesus, and watch and listen for what Jesus does and says. Receive his healing love.

(11) Sometimes we forgive someone who has sinned against us, but we still need to grieve the hurt. Other times, to forgive the rest of the "five gallons," we need to grieve so we realize what we have lost. Look at some of the people you need to forgive. Are there hurts in the relationships that you still need to grieve? Ask the Lord for insight. Journal any of the hurts you need to grieve. Try to jot down your feelings, the things the offense cost you. What did you lose? Innocence, reputation, dignity, respect, finances, trust? More? Get beyond the surface emotions. For example, sometimes I feel anger when someone says something rude and offensive to me. But anger is a secondary emotion. What's underneath that anger? Is there hurt? Embarrassment? Shame? Humiliation? Rejection? Abandonment? Get specific, and grieve what you are experiencing. Then willingly leave it with the God of the cross. Jesus took up your sin, and their sin; He took up your hurt and their hurt. Release it all to Him as you grieve. For more help grieving, you may want to look at the resources listed in Exercise 13 below.

(12) You may want to pray some Psalms to help you grieve. About 40 percent of the Psalms are lament psalms in which the psalmist is processing negative emotions, grief, hurt, and the like. Often what I do is skim through some psalms until I find one that resonates with my emotional state of being, and I linger there and pray that psalm back to God through my own words and circumstances. I have found this to be an extremely helpful process. One of the beautiful things about the psalmists is they do not get stuck in sadness; they look up and out of their grief to God in faith and surrender. This is essential for processing. Remember, your goal is to process your pain and to forgive those who sin against you.

(13) You may want to access some other resources to help you process your grief. In my book *River Dwellers*, in chapter 5: Twists in the River Bend, I talk a great deal about grief and "soul-robbing disappointments." This is a helpful chapter to read when you are processing grief and disappointments. Also, in my book *Calm in the Storm*, chapter 3: Drawing Near to God, I have an entire section on grieving. My book *The Soul Care Leader* also has two helpful chapters for processing grief—chapter 2: A Healthy Leader has some strong insights; and Chapter 6: Talking Versus Processing is particularly helpful for processing difficult issues. This chapter has an entire section on grief. Add further thoughts, perhaps produced from these chapters, here.

(14) Look at some of the hurts that you have forgiven. How has God redeemed some of these hardships and hurts in your life? If you are living through some that have not yet been redeemed, meditate on and claim the promises in Romans 8:28-39 and James 1:2-8. God promises that He will redeem all hardships that come into our lives to make us more like Jesus, and to make us whole and complete, lacking nothing. He also promises that if we do not know how He can redeem a particular crisis, we can ask Him for wisdom, and He will show us. Take time to ask God for wisdom about how He can redeem these hardships in your life. You will grow and benefit more through the hardships if you know how God is trying to redeem them in your life. This will also empower you with hope, which can enable you to let go of the power that anger is feeding you. Often when I have asked God to show me how He can redeem a crisis in my life, it has taken time. I have had to persist in asking, at times, for six months before God made it clear to me. And yet, He has always showed me how He can redeem the crisis if I have persisted in asking in faith (as James instructs).

Notes

Notes

Seven

HEALING WOUNDS

Preparation work for this chapter:

Read *Soul Care* Principle #5: Healing Wounds

In the video series, watch: Healing Wounds

In the Soul Care eCourse, watch lessons 24-27

Summary of Soul Care Principle #5: Healing Wounds

Everyone is wounded. It is only a matter of degrees, by how much. Sometimes an emotional wound is like a splinter. Imagine I had a splinter in my thumb, and it was infected, and you came up to me and bumped into my thumb. How would I respond? I would have a disproportionate reaction to the impact. In the same way, some people are carrying around infected splinters in their soul, and when people bump up against them, they overreact. The overreaction is indicative of unhealed wounding. Other people don't overreact; they underreact. They are more like a leper. A leper loses feeling in his or her extremities to the point that they can put their hand on a hot stove and not feel pain. Some people have been wounded in such a way that it has cauterized their emotional nerve endings. Often, we are so used to our wounding that we think, *Well, that's just the way I am.* But this isn't true; we have been wounded, and our hurts and pains have caused us to become like this. We need healing.

The good news is Jesus didn't just die on the cross to forgive our sin; He also died to heal our wounds. Isaiah 53:4, 5: "Surely he took up our pain and bore our suffering, yet we considered him punished by God, stricken by him, and afflicted. But he was pierced for our transgressions, he was crushed for our iniquities; the punishment that brought us peace was on him, and by his wounds we are healed." When Jesus died on the cross, He took up our pain and bore the suffering our pain has caused us. The things you have suffered in your lifetime, Jesus suffered with you on the cross.

God promises that He can redeem everything that comes into our lives to make us more like Jesus. It isn't that He brought it into our lives or caused it, but that He is so good that, even when evil touches your life, when God touches that evil, He can make good come from it. Romans 8:28, 29: "And we know that in all things God works for the good of those who love him, who have been called according to his purpose. For those God foreknew he also predestined to be conformed to the likeness of his Son." James has a similar thought in the first chapter of his epistle. He tells us that we should rejoice during our trials because God can redeem them to make us whole, complete, lacking nothing. He adds that if we don't know how God can redeem trials to make us like Jesus, we should ask God for wisdom, and He will tell us. So whenever I go through suffering, I claim these passages and ask God how He can redeem this difficulty to make me like Jesus. I persist in asking until I see how God can redeem it, how He is trying to make me more like Jesus through this difficulty. Then I surrender to his shaping hand.

Whenever a wound has been caused by someone else, we are also going to have to go back and forgive that person. But even if we have already forgiven them, the wound can leave lasting impact, and we need healing to be made whole. In my own journey, I realized that I had some unprocessed wounds from my childhood. I didn't have the ability as a child to process those things, so when Jen and I hit a marriage crisis, I had to go back to some of my childhood hurts to process them in Jesus' healing presence so I could become more like Jesus and be made more whole and healthier in my relational interactions. My wounds were contributing to my dysfunction and causing us problems, and Jen had things from her past that she needed healing from as well.

We have to keep our relationship with God at the forefront of our healing journey. Many people start to feel a little better, and they stop pressing in and pressing through because they have the wrong goal.

I went back and talked to my family about many things, but I didn't do it to blame them. I did it to take responsibility for my life and experience more freedom and fullness. I wanted to honor my family, but the most honorable thing I could do was break free.

How do we access Jesus' healing for our souls? Let me provide a few big principles that can help.

Big principle #1: God isn't trying to fix us; He wants a relationship with us. Often when we are carrying pain from our past, we are desperate for God to take it away. We want Him to fix us; we want Him to alleviate our symptoms and remove our pain. But it is in relationship with God that healing occurs. We have to keep our relationship with God at the forefront of our healing journey. Many people start to feel a little better, and they stop pressing in and pressing through because they have the wrong goal. Their goal is simply to alleviate symptoms and feel better. But our true goal is to know and be like Jesus. Hold fast to that goal.

Big principle #2: Theology 101: God is smart, and He knows stuff we don't know, and if we let Him, He likes to tell us. God knows what memories from your past need to be touched with his healing presence. God knows how to heal those things. We need to look to Him throughout the healing journey and trust Him to lead us to freedom and fullness. Ask the Holy Spirit to show you what memories need to be addressed, and ask Him to lead you down the right healing path for those things.

Big principle #3: Tell me your story. When people come looking for help, they usually come with a presenting problem—like anxiety, depression, addiction, a marriage problem, and the like. But the presenting problem is usually a symptom; it is not the disease. If we are going to get healthy, we have to get to the root issues. The roots are always tied to our story. No one becomes who they are without having lived the life they have lived. So I always begin by asking people to tell me their story. You tell me your story, I will tell you your issues. If you tell me only your issues, I guarantee you it is connected to your story.

Big principle #4: Only God heals the soul. The key to healing is to get people into the presence of Jesus. Jesus is the healer. My goal, when I pray for someone, is simply to bring them to Jesus. So I want to listen for the Holy Spirit's directions, insights, and revelations, because He knows how to lead people to Jesus for healing. I will tell you the most common approach to inner healing, to healing the heart and soul from our past hurts and wounds, but I will also tell you upfront that I don't use this approach unless the Holy Spirit leads me to do so. I believe the Holy Spirit is creative in his healing approach. Here is the most common approach: as you enter into a memory that needs healing, you recall all the sights, sounds, smells, and emotions, and then you invite Jesus into the memory. If you are praying with someone, they will usually say something like this: "Jesus is always with you. He was with you when this happened. Let's pray you see Jesus in this memory. Where is Jesus? What is He doing? Watch and listen; watch what Jesus does, listen to what Jesus says." Then they pray that the Holy Spirit would show them Jesus. I have seen Jesus use this approach to bring his presence to bear on a wounded soul to great effect. I'm not at all against it; I just rely on the Holy Spirit to lead me for my own healing and when I am praying for the healing of those around me. It is just one of many approaches He can use.

One of the things that does seem to be common in healing memories is that God uses pictures; He uses the sanctified imagination. I think this is because most of our memories are stored in pictures, and when God brings healing, He often uses prophetic images to release his healing presence. Acts 2:17, 18: "In the last days, God says, I will pour out my Spirit on all people. Your sons and daughters will prophesy, your young men will see visions, your old men will dream dreams. Even on my servants, both men and women, I will pour out my Spirit in those days, and they will prophesy." This promise is for the "last days," which, biblically, is from the time Jesus rose from the grave until He returns. So this means it is for us because we are in this period of time known as the last days. God promises that He will pour out his Spirit and people will hear his voice—specifically, through dreams and visions.

I don't get a lot of dreams and visions or pictures from God; probably only 10 percent of what I receive from the Lord prophetically comes through dreams and visions. But the time I am most likely to receive a picture is for inner healing—whether for me or for someone else. Many times I have received a dream that produced healing for me, or I have received an image when I was praying for someone who needed inner healing.

There are three blocks to receiving inner healing that are common; I will mention them here. First, some people struggle to receive from the Lord because of introspection. Introspection is an eyes-on-me, heady approach to faith. We analyze things rather than receiving them by faith. So when the Lord speaks, we begin to question: "Is that God? Is that me? How can I tell? I don't want to be wrong." And we literally talk ourselves out of faith. This is rooted in pride; we are making life too much about us. We need to repent of pride and begin to learn how to walk by faith and receive humbly from the Lord. Part of being humble is the need to test prophecy (1 Thessalonians 5:19-21). I talk about hearing God's voice—the biblical word for that is prophecy—in my book *River Dwellers*. You may want to read that specific chapter for more help.

Second, sometimes people are blocked in receiving inner healing because of shame. Often what happens with this person is they enter into some memory from their past that needs to be healed, and they can see the memory, they feel some emotion, but they will say, "I can't see Jesus" or "I can only see his feet; I can't see his face." This is pretty common, and it is the result of shame. They carry shame because of what they have done or because of what has been done to them, and they won't look at Jesus' face because they feel unworthy. But shame is just pride wrapped in self-disgust; once again, we are making life too much about us. We need to humble ourselves and realize that Jesus' love is not just for others. It is for us too. And we need to exercise our will and look up to Jesus.

Third, some people get hindered in the healing journey because of a demonic block. They go into the memory that needs healing, they can see the sights and feel the emotions, but when they invite Jesus to come with healing love, the memory disappears. It evaporates and the scene goes blank, or it goes to darkness. That, most often, is a demonic block, which we will address in the last principle.

Healing wounds is not a formula. We need to follow the Spirit's direction and leadings. Sometimes He may lead you to a specific memory, and Jesus' presence may be revealed or made known to you in some healing way. But this is only one approach. Sometimes He may just lead you to meditate on a passage of Scripture. I have seen people experience God's healing through a revelatory encounter with the Spirit in the Word. Trust the Lord and follow the promptings of the Spirit.

Sometimes significant healing can come through an encounter with God. We all want the big zap! We want to have an encounter with God that heals all our wounds, and one day that *will* happen . . . when we die! When we meet Him face to face, we will be like Him, but in the meantime, we are on a journey toward freedom and fullness, wholeness and healing. And sometimes on this journey, God chooses to heal us not with an encounter but with his tenderness over time. I believe there are some wounds that God cannot heal with his power in a moment, but only with his tenderness over time. We need to trust God in how He chooses to heal us; He knows best.

I believe there are some wounds that God cannot heal with his power in a moment, but only with his tenderness over time. We need to trust God in how He chooses to heal us; He knows best.

One of the ways that God has used to heal me over time is through redemptive suffering. In redemptive suffering I sit with the Lord with some pain or hurt from my soul, and I feel the pain and grief, but I also focus on his presence. It is like two streams are running within me: there is one stream, of the hurt; and there is a second stream, of his loving presence. Often, as I sit there, I experience tears of sadness or grief, and I experience the peace and love of Jesus welling up within me. For some of the hurts I have experienced in life, the Lord has led me to sit with Him in redemptive suffering over several months until, finally, the tears dried up and the hurt was healed.

I find it is always helpful to journal on these healing encounters. Write down your experiences with God. You are creating a personal history with God, and these healing events in your life develop deeper levels of trust in your relationship with God, so we want to be careful to catalogue and remember them.

Healing is not a panacea for all that ails us. Sometimes we've experienced some tremendous healing in our relationship with God, but we still have some aftereffects of the trauma and wounds in our life. There may be some leftover angst or some other similar symptom. It's okay; trust God and keep doing the right thing.

There is one last thing I want to mention. We have to fight our base instinct to resist God. When I entered into the healing journey, I found I had resistance to the Holy Spirit that I had to identify and surrender. I was resistant to some things, like inner healing, because they were outside of the church experiences in which I grew up. I found there were other things I was resistant to because I didn't trust God. And still other things I resisted because God was calling me to do something hard, and I didn't want to do it—like confess something to another person. But our resistance isn't tied to authentic humility. Resistance is most often linked to pride, and God opposes the proud. We need to humble ourselves before the Lord if we want to experience his healing grace. Fight your base instinct to resist the Holy Spirit.

Experiences

(1) **What are some of the major wounds in your life? How do these wounds continue to negatively impact and limit you? Ask the Lord to show you areas that need healing. Let Him bring to the surface memories that need his healing touch. Journal on the wounds, how they were formed, and any healing encounters you have with God as you pray. You may want to discuss how these wounds impact you with other people who know you well and know your story. Get their perspective. Come humbly and ask for their input. (Note: feel free to use the space below to jot down a reminder of the memory that needs to be addressed, but it will not be adequate to write the narrative. You will want to keep a separate journal of some type.)**

(2) **"Sooner or later we have to take responsibility for the baggage we carry, and we have to process it, and then we can receive healing. . . . That means you must face your past, and you must process the events of your past that have contributed to your present broken ways" (*Soul Care*, 2016, p. 154). Often people say to me, "Do I have to go there?" Or, "I'm afraid to go back into my past; I'm afraid I will start crying and never stop." Or sometimes people say, "I think I was abused, but I'm not sure. I don't want to know. Do I have to know?" What feelings arise at the thought of facing past events or exploring painful memories? The Kingdom of God is a kingdom of light, not darkness. There is no healing in the darkness. It takes courage to face our past, and often we need help from others to go there. With the help**

of your group, the Holy Spirit, and any professionals you may need, face your past and find the healing Jesus offers. What issues of your past are you reluctant to face? What issues have you acknowledged but not really processed? Ask God to show you, and don't resist what the Holy Spirit reveals.

(3) Ask the Lord to show you the shields you have relied on to cope with your pain and hurt. What self-protections do you use? What defense mechanisms have you relied on to cope? Your self-life is most strongly formed in your greatest area of childhood wounding. Your self-life is the part of you that is self-reliant, self-dependent, self-protective, self-centered, self-fortified, and sometimes just plain selfish. What was your greatest childhood wounding, and how was your self-life formed in it? How does it continue to manifest in your life?

(4) Ask the Lord to bring you through your story. Think through your life on a timeline, walk through your life slowly with God, and ask Him to show you the major highs and lows, the peaks and valleys, and if there are specific things from your past He needs to address, speak into, and heal. Think of your life in sections: preschool, elementary school, junior high, high school, college, etc. Slowly walk through each time frame and ask the Lord to show you any specific memories from that time that He wants to speak to you about, touch, heal, and address. What does God bring to your attention? Don't ignore it; allow Him to bring to the surface important memories. What memories does He bring to your mind and highlight? You may want to set aside a day to walk through your life with God, or you may do this slowly with God in your regular time with Him. One by one, bring these memories to God for his healing.

(5) Set aside some time to pray through wounds with a trusted small group. You can either go on a retreat with your friends to pray through your lives together, or you can bring the major events of your lives to each other and pray through those memories together. After presenting your wounds to one another, talk less, pray less words, and listen more for the Spirit's insight and direction. Wait on the Lord on behalf of each other.

(6) If you are new to inner healing, you can use this as a guide. It is not meant to be a formula, just a helpful guide for people who are newly venturing into this. Enter the memory and recall all that you can: the sights, sounds, smells, feelings, the words spoken. Invite the Lord to reveal Himself to you in the memory. Ask Jesus: can you please give me a sense of your presence in that event? Watch and listen. Notice what Jesus does, what He says, notice his emotions. Also, ask the Lord to show you what you came to believe as a result of this event. Are there any lies that were formed in this? What is the truth? If it is hard for you to do this alone, you may want to do this with trusted friends.

(7) Read through the chapter on the prophetic, on hearing God's voice, in *River Dwellers*. Hearing God is vital for intimacy with Him, for insight into our journey, for healing our wounds, and for helping those around us encounter the Lord's presence. Ask the Lord to help you become more sensitive to his presence and to the leadings and promptings of the Spirit. Develop a "listening journal." Spend regular time every day in quiet for a few minutes and ask the Holy Spirit to speak to you. Write down what you sense the Lord saying to you and test it with Scripture and with other godly friends who have a track record of hearing God's voice.

(8) Where do you tend to overreact? What are your trigger points of overreaction? What emotions do you tend to feel when you overreact? What happened in your past that caused you to be overreactive? Ask the people around you, and don't defend yourself. Where do you underreact? Again, get feedback from others without being defensive. Are there any emotions you don't feel, that you are out of touch with? What happened in your past that caused the underreaction? Often the areas where we overreact or underreact are indicative of unhealed wounds in our soul. Ask the Lord to show you any areas where you have symptomatic ex-

pressions of unaddressed wounding. Why do you do what you do? Why do you feel what you feel? What wounding in your life led to these over/under reactions?

(9) If you are going through painful things in your life right now, spend some time meditating on Romans 8:28-39 and James 1:1-5. Ask the Lord how He can redeem these trials and difficulties in your life to make you more like Jesus. Persist in asking until it becomes clear how God is trying to form Christ in you through this trial. Surrender what you need to surrender. Trust God where you need to trust Him. How is God going to redeem this in your life and form Christ in you? Cooperate with the work of the Spirit in any way you can. What does it look like for you to entrust this pain to God?

(10) As God has surfaced wounds and is bringing healing, is there anyone you need to forgive? Sometimes as we process our wounds, we discover that we may have some people that we thought we had completely forgiven, but we still have a full two gallons left in the tank to forgive. Ask the Holy Spirit to show you if there are people connected to these wounds that you need to forgive to a greater extent.

(11) Sometimes people tell me their story, but it doesn't match the level of pain or dysfunction they are carrying. I can tell something is missing. They may not be completely honest about their story because they are self-protecting, or perhaps they are protecting their family image. Or they may not know some of the story—there may be some missing pieces, perhaps that the family has not told them. As you look at your life, and your story, do the pieces match? Does your level of pain and brokenness match the story that you tell? Ask the people in your small group or the people who are closest to you for their feedback. Do you need to have any follow-up conversations with your family to help fill in some of the pieces to the story? Who do you need to talk to? What do you need to ask them?

(12) Is there any place in your story where the Lord wants you to spend time in redemptive suffering? It isn't an encounter that you need, but you need healing over time with God's tender love. Ask the Lord for revelation about this, and then spend time with Him soaking in his presence. Feel the pain, the rejection, and the hurt, and feel his tender love. Do the work of grieving, and let Him bring healing to your soul over time.

(13) Sit with the Lord in your pain and consciously focus on his loving presence. You can use a phrase like, "He restores my soul" as you sit in silence. If your mind wanders, bring it back to focus on the Lord's presence by repeating the phrase. Don't meditate on the phrase to understand it; rather, meditate on the phrase to experience his restorative presence. Give Him access to your pain and rest in his restorative presence for as long as it takes. There are some things He can heal only with his tenderness over time.

Notes

Notes

Eight

OVERCOMING FEARS

Preparation work for this chapter:

Read *Soul Care* Principle #6: Overcoming Fears

In the Soul Care Video series, watch: Overcoming Fears

In the Soul Care eCourse, watch lessons 28-31

Summary of Soul Care Principle #6: Overcoming Fears

The most-used command in the Bible is "Fear not." Often it comes with a promise: "Fear not! For I am with you." This is why we do not need to be afraid, because God is with us. God says this more than anything else in Scripture. The problem is that fear often causes us to sin and rebel against God.

Think about the impact of fear on people in the Bible. God promised the nation of Israel property: the Promised Land. It was Moses' generation that was to inherit the land; this was the generation that God had chosen, the leader God had appointed, and the time God had determined for the inheritance. But fear caused an entire generation of people to miss out on their prophetic destiny! That's the power of fear. This is why God says, so often, "Do not be afraid."

Think about King Saul. He is a unique man in history; he inaugurates a kingdom. Not many people in history are in position to establish a kingdom—many inherit one, some usurp one, but Saul establishes a kingdom. And yet, Saul had a problem with fear. When he goes to his first battle, fear causes him to rebel against God and do what was forbidden and perform a sacrifice. He was told to wait for Samuel, the priest, to come and offer the sacrifice, but the troops were leaving because they were terrified of the enemy, and Saul chose to act on fear, and thus rebelled against God.

And, in the end, his fear costs him his kingdom. His kingdom is torn from him and handed to a man after God's own heart, David. Fear cost a man and his entire lineage their prophetic destiny.

Think about King Ahaz. In Isaiah 7:1-17, King Rezin of Aram and King Pekah of Israel team up together to attack King Ahaz and the people of Judah; this is something like the two big kids on the block picking on the little kid. The people, and the leaders of Judah, are terrified. So God sends them a prophetic word through the prophet Isaiah: "Be careful, keep calm, and don't be afraid" (Isaiah 7:4). But God doesn't just speak these words, He also offers Ahaz practical help. He invites Ahaz to ask for a sign, to bolster his trust, to show him that God will deliver him and his people. Sadly, Ahaz refuses to ask for a sign because he has already made up his mind to rebel against God! God gives him a sign anyway. "The virgin will conceive and give birth to a son, and will call him Immanuel" (Isaiah 7:14). We know this as a Messianic promise, but most scholars—and I agree with them—believe there was a fulfillment of this prophecy in Isaiah's day as well. A barren woman conceived; many believe it was Isaiah's wife who was barren and conceived. And it acted as a sign to the people of God that God could deliver a barren, powerless nation from the grip of its enemies.

I think the number one question for God on the heart of most people is this: "Do you love me?" And I think God's response is: "I have sent my Son, Immanuel, to die for you; I am with you. I've proven my love." And the number one question from God to us is, "Now will you trust me?" Biblically speaking, the opposite of faith is not doubt. The opposite of faith is unbelief that leads to disobedience. The problem with fear is that it often stirs us to unbelief, and that leads people to rebel and disobey God. This is why we must process our fear. "We can either act on fear or we can act on faith, but we cannot act on both. We can feel afraid and act on faith, but we can't act on both. We must choose" (*Soul Care*, 2016, p. 187).

Behind our sin, unnoticed, often lurks fear. God notices this, of course, and He calls us to trust Him. David was an unusually soul-savvy individual. In Psalm 139:23, 24, David prays, "Search me, O God, and know my heart, test me and know my anxious thoughts. See if there is any offensive way in me, and lead me in the way everlasting." Notice that before David prays that God would show him if there is any sin in his life, David prays that God would show him if there is any fear, or any anxious thoughts, because David knew it was his fear that often led him to disobey God.

The good news is that Jesus has promised us peace so we can overcome our fear. In John 14:27, Jesus said, "Peace I leave with you; my peace I give you. I do not give to you as the world gives. Do not let your hearts be troubled, and do not be afraid." Jesus offers us his peace; He is the Prince of Peace. Jesus offers us a peace that comes from Heaven. It is not a peace rooted in earth's circumstances or earth's resources. It is an eternal peace that flows from the heart of God. The Bible refers to this as a peace that passes human understanding; it is a supernatural peace that defies logic. This peace is available to us.

One of the problems with fear is we are often tempted to manipulate and control others when we are afraid. When Jen and I went through our marriage crisis, in the beginning she often felt smothered by me; this was because I was so urgent about fixing the problems. It was fear driving me, even though, at the time, I didn't realize it. Often parents are motivated by fear for their children and thus resort to control. Religion is rooted in fear, and legalism is a fear-based attempt to control people's behaviors. With legalism we modify the holiness standard of God because of our fears. God says, for example, that we cannot be drunk. But the legalist is afraid that if people drink, they will get drunk, that they can't merely trust God's standard, so they up the ante and say, "No drinking, in Jesus' name!"

Ultimately, to conquer our fears, we must become aware of our fears, surrender our fears to God, and learn how to truly trust God. Sadly, sometimes we have the right words, words that sound like faith, but our actions betray that we do not really have active, authentic trust in God. It is a passive, religious faith that is on display.

> Believing that God is redemptive is critically important to developing true faith.

Believing that God is redemptive is critically important to developing true faith. God never promises us that everything will work out in this world. Jesus told us that in this world we would have trouble, but He also told us that we don't need to be afraid because He has overcome the world. Our trust isn't supposed to be that everything will work out. Our trust is that Jesus has overcome, that He is with us, and that He can redeem everything that comes into our lives to make us more like Himself. Ultimately, we don't have to be fearful because we trust that He has gone to prepare a place for us where all the evils of the world will be vanquished and those who follow Him will be rewarded for their faithful trust.

Our fears are often connected to our wounds. When a situation in our present arises that reminds us of a situation in our past, it triggers us, and we are often afraid. But it is important to realize that God often brings us into present situations that trigger our past wounds. He isn't doing this to be cruel; He is doing this to lead us to heal the past and help us develop true trust in Him, a trust that will allow us to overcome in the present. In my case, I had a fear of not being loved, and when Jen and I hit that marriage snag the person I loved most in the world no longer loved me. It triggered my fear of not being loved, and yet it was the very thing I needed to address the issues of my heart and soul and to seek God for healing.

We seek to defend ourselves from our fears; we put up shields of anger, power, control, manipulation, or passive-aggressive behavior, and we find ourselves running, fleeing, and hiding. But if we are going to learn how to trust God and walk in victory, we need to lay down these shields and rely on God. I had to become aware of some of the symptomatic expressions of fear in my life for the simple reason that I did not feel afraid. Now, please hear me: I am not saying that I was not afraid. I simply didn't feel the emotion of fear. When I was afraid, most often I felt anger. I felt a sense of power; the adrenaline rush in my body produced a sense of power within me that, sadly, masked my fear. I had to figure out some of the physiological responses I had to fear. My heart rate ticked up a notch, and I could feel a little inner tension in my chest. My mind quickened and raced and I felt a little tinge of anxiety (I lost my peace). I had to realize that these were the symptoms of fear so that, rather than acting on my fear, I could turn to God, process my fear, and learn to truly trust Him.

It helps to identify your fears. What is your root fear? People often ask me for a list of root fears, but the issue is not that difficult. Look at your story. If it were someone else's story, given what happened in their life, what do you think they would be afraid of? Ask a few others to weigh in. You'll probably figure it out pretty quickly. My root fear is the fear of not being loved—that was the big tree in my garden—and when Jen no longer loved me, it was the very thing I needed to address this root fear I had been unaware of. This is why God brings us face to face with our fears: so that we will learn to surrender, access his healing, and deepen our faith. He doesn't want us to live with unprocessed, unhealed wounds our entire life.

Once you identify your fears, and the manifestations of those fears (like anxiety, or little phrases running through your head like "I don't care what people think"), these become your indicator clues to turn to God in trusting dependence. In the past, at times when someone was upset with me, I would have imaginary conversations with the person. I would think about what I was going to say, and what they were going to say, and I would play out a conversation in my head before ever sitting down to talk to the person. But all that did was feed my fear. So I made a choice: imaginary conversations were illegal for me, and I refused to allow myself to continue to go there. Instead, I would reinforce my identity in Christ that I was deeply loved by God. I would tell myself the truth: that I wanted this person to like me, but even if they didn't like me, Jesus' love was enough for me. And I would stop the imaginary conversations from fueling the fire of fear in my heart.

I made a choice: imaginary conversations were illegal for me, and I refused to allow myself to continue to go there. Instead, I would reinforce my identity in Christ.

How do we overcome fear? Let's look at the Apostle Paul's advice in Philippians 4:4-7: "Rejoice in the Lord always. I will say it again: Rejoice! Let your gentleness be evident to all. The Lord is near. Do not be anxious about anything, but in everything, by prayer and petition, with thanksgiving, present your requests to God. And the peace of God, which transcends all understanding, will guard your hearts and your minds in Christ Jesus."

First, *we should begin with worship.* Paul says, "Rejoice in the Lord always. I will say it again: Rejoice!" The reason Paul desired to say this again is because he was always using this word! Our natural inclination is to think: "Paul didn't really mean that." But then you look at Paul's life and see him get beat up in prison, and the first thing he does is to worship. Paul meant it! "There are only two times to worship: when we feel like it, and when we don't. And when we don't feel like it is the time we need it most" (*Soul Care*, 2016, p. 196). When I went through the marriage crisis with Jen, every night we were having conversations about the conflict, trying to resolve it. And I would leave every conversation feeling anxious. But after we talked, I went upstairs and sat alone with God and worshiped. I often worshiped for an hour or more, and as I got my eyes off myself, off our circumstances, and put my eyes on Jesus, I could feel the peace of Heaven returning to my soul.

Second, *choose a gentle response.* "Let your gentleness be evident to all" (Philippians 4:5). The word gentleness is rooted in the words submission and meekness. God is calling us to slow down and not act impulsively. When we are afraid, adrenaline surges in our bodies, and that feeling and emotion calls us to act quickly. In Psalm 46:10, the psalmist writes, "Be still, and know that I am God." But the context is a time of trouble (Psalm 46:1). He chooses the opposite response to the adrenaline surge in his body. Rather than speeding up and acting hastily, he chooses to slow down and center on God and take a careful, centered course of action. This is brilliant soul advice.

Third, *remember the Lord's presence, and fix your eyes on Jesus.* "The Lord is near. Do not be anxious." This is the center of the whole passage; the reason we do not need to be afraid is because the Lord is nearby. This is the promise God always gives His people when He tells them not to be afraid: "For I am with you." We all suffer from what I call "mind drift." Mind drift simply means that our minds naturally drift toward our greatest pressing problem because of fear. If your greatest pressing problem is a work problem, finance problem, or marriage problem, if you let your mind go and you aren't intentionally focused on anything, your mind will naturally drift toward that problem. That is the power of fear. "Peace is a by-product of fixing our mind on Jesus" (*Soul Care*, 2016, p. 198).

Mind drift simply means that our minds naturally drift toward our greatest pressing problem because of fear.

Fourth, *overcoming your fears will involve redemptive suffering.* As we mentioned earlier, our fears are often connected to wounds. While we are in the presence of Jesus, we can bring our wounds of the past, and our wounds of the present, to Jesus for his healing touch. In seasons of intense pain or crisis, I often practice ten-minute retreats. I sit with the Lord quietly, feel the pain, feel his loving presence, and allow Him to heal the pain. As the wounds are healed, it is much easier to live at peace.

Fifth, *overcoming your fears will involve surrender.* There is no peace without surrender. We must choose to trust God with a real, authentic, active faith. "Peace is often a by-product of a fully surrendered heart. It is the simplicity of trust, and the sweetness of surrender, that leads us to peace in the inmost place" (*Soul Care*, 2016, p. 199).

Sixth, *overcoming fears always involves action.* James said that faith without deeds is dead. True faith leads to obedient action. We have to courageously do the right thing even if we still feel afraid.

Experiences

(1) What are some of the fears you wrestle with? How does fear manifest in your life? When your fears get tapped, what do you experience physically, emotionally, viscerally? Do you struggle with mind drift? Does your mind race? Are you tempted to have imaginary conversations? Do you struggle with fight, flight, or freeze? What does fear cause you to avoid? When you are afraid, what are the physiological symptoms you experience? Journal your thoughts and emotions here.

(2) "The number one question in the heart of people for God is, 'Do you love me?' And the number one question in the heart of God for people is, 'Will you trust me?'" *(Soul Care,* 2016, p. 186). Where do you struggle to trust God? What causes you to be worried, anxious, or afraid? How can you develop authentic trust? You may want to read my books *Deep Faith* and *Authentic* to help you develop an active trust in God rather than a passive faith that doesn't produce peace.

(3) "We can either act on fear or we can act on faith, but we cannot act on both. . . . When fear lurks in your heart unattended, it is bound to cost you immeasurably" (*Soul Care*, 2016, p. 187). In what situations do you tend to act on fear? In what ways has fear cost you? How has it cost your family? Where is fear threatening to rob you of your prophetic destiny?

(4) What is/are your root fear(s)? Look at your story. Look at your family history. Reflect on the hurts and wounds in your life. Can you connect the dots? Can you see how these elements of your story have clearly contributed to your root fears? Ask others in your group, who know you and know your story, for insights.

(5) What are the phrases that run through your head when you are afraid? Pay close attention. Ask the Lord for insight and revelation. As you go through your day and fear gets triggered, pay attention to your thoughts. Monitor your self-talk. What are the imaginary conversations you have in your head? What do you say to yourself, about yourself? How do you prop up your fears? Journal some of that here.

(6) How are your fears connected to your wounds and hurts? How has God brought you face to face with your fears? How is He doing that at this point in your life? How are the current situations you face connected to the wounds of your past? Are you using this as a redemptive opportunity to heal the wounds of your past and present and learning to trust God with an active, authentic faith?

(7) What self-protective measures do you use when you are afraid? What shields do you rely on? How are those shields preventing you from trusting God? The problem with shields is they are indiscriminate; they not only attempt to block out the things we are afraid of, they also block God from healing us. How are your shields preventing you from God's healing?

(8) Too often in hardship we ask God the wrong question. We ask Him, "Why?" We need to ask, "How?" How can God redeem this situation as He has promised (Romans 8:28-39; James 1:1-5)? The "why" question often undermines my trust, but when I start asking God how He can redeem something, it fills me with hope. Where have you been asking God "why"? Shift your question to: "How can you redeem this, God?" Ask God to show you how He can redeem a present situation to form Christ in you. How can you cooperate with God in that maturation process? Persist in pursuing God until the answer begins to emerge, and cooperate fully with God in the process of His redeeming work.

(9) How are your fears connected to the lies you believe? Look back over your reflections about the three big lies: people-pleasing, performance, and control. When you are standing on that faulty foundation, how does it trigger fear in you? All three lies have impacted my life, and I have a different reaction to different lies. (For me, fear is more likely to manifest as anxiety on the people-pleasing lie, but it is more likely to display as anger when I am wrestling with control.) Journal how these lies affect your fears.

(10) What courageous action steps do you need to take to overcome your fears? Often our fear causes us to avoid circumstances and conversations we need to address. If we continue to allow our fear to rule and dictate our choices, we will not overcome our fears. Where have you allowed fear to dictate your choices? Where is God inviting you into a courageous choice that will help you trust Him and overcome fear? Prayerfully consider this, and then courageously follow through.

(11) What do you need to surrender? There is no peace without surrender. Sometimes we say the right words, we speak words of trust, but the reality is we haven't really surrendered because the supernatural peace of Christ has not yet been imparted. For example, in 2017 my family was moving to New York, to a lower-paying job in an area with a higher cost of living. I was going to spend more time traveling, speaking, doing conferences, and writing. But I also didn't know that invites would come sufficiently enough to provide for our needs. I felt fear. I had to surrender and trust God. I knew I had surrendered the issue when I felt the fear lift. Journal the areas you need to surrender.

(12) In John 14:27, Jesus said, "Peace I leave with you; my peace I give you. I do not give to you as the world gives. Do not let your hearts be troubled and do not be afraid." Jesus is the Prince of Peace. Jesus is never nervous. I realize that in my life the only time I lose my peace is when I am out of alignment with Jesus, because Jesus has not lost his peace, and He has promised to give me his perfect peace. Anxiety, therefore, has become a gift to me. It is one of the early warning signs that something is "off" in my soul; I am out of alignment with Christ. I go to Jesus, ask Him to show me what is out of alignment, process it, and his peace returns. Meditate on John 14:27 over the next days (or weeks) if fear is a significant issue in your life. What is the Lord showing you? What is He revealing to you? Where are things

"off" in your soul or out of alignment with God? What do you need to process? What do you need to let go? What do you need to surrender? What robs you of your peace? Bring your fears to Jesus. What is He saying to you?

(13) Philippians promises us a peace that passes understanding. Paul wrote that thought from prison! Recall times in your life when you have experienced the supernatural peace of God that passes understanding. Write some of these down. These are part of your personal history with God.

(14) 1 John 4:16-18: "And so we know and rely on the love God has for us. God is love. Whoever lives in love lives in God, and God in them. This is how love is made complete among us so that we will have confidence on the day of judgment: in this world we are like Jesus. There is no fear in love. But perfect love drives out fear, because fear has to do with punishment. The one who fears is not made perfect in love." John says that we know and rely on the love God has for us. One of the great problems with Western Christianity is it is too cognitive; it is far too often a knowledge-based discipleship approach. We have wrongly assumed that if we believe the right things, we will do the right things. But that isn't true. Knowing that God loves us is a good starting point, but we have to learn how to rely on the love of God. When we do, perfect love will drive out fear. John says that "the one who fears is not made perfect in love." If we are still afraid, love has not been perfected in us, and we have not really learned how to rely on God's love. Meditate on this passage over the next few days or weeks. Ask the Lord for insight and revelation. Ask the Lord to show you how you can rely on his love day by day, circumstance by circumstance. What is the Lord showing you? What is He revealing to you—about yourself? About Him? Use this space to write what He is showing you.

(15) Review some of the Old Testament stories I mentioned at the start of this chapter: the Israelites missing out on the Promised Land, Saul's kingdom being taken from him, and King Ahaz in Isaiah 7. Spend time reflecting on these accounts. Pray through them. Ask the Lord for insights into your own soul, and for your own family. How has fear thwarted you from God's purposes, God's destiny, in your life? Where do you need to repent and make course corrections? How big a role has fear played in your life and in the life of your family members? Ask God for insight, and write about that here.

(16) Not everything in this world will work out. Ultimately, we can't conquer our fears without factoring in eternity. Jesus has gone before us to prepare a place for us. In Heaven there will be no more sickness, no more death, no more sin, no more temptation, no more injustice, and no longer any form of evil. To live in peace through tumultuous times, we need to sink deep roots in our eternal citizenship. Mediate on Philippians 1:12-26. Paul is in prison, and there are people who are preaching the gospel under false pretenses; they are preaching so Paul will be punished more. But Paul says that doesn't matter to him so long as the gospel gets preached! He is unrattled by his predicament because he knows if he lives, he lives for Christ; but if he dies, he gains Jesus and Heaven. It is his eternal perspective that so often helps him live at peace in terrible times. You may want to go back to passages about your identity and do more identity work. You may also want to meditate on 2 Corinthians 4:7-18. Journal more of these thoughts here.

Notes

Notes

Nine

DELIVERANCE

Preparation work for this chapter:

Read *Soul Care* Principle #7: Deliverance

In the Soul Care Video series, watch: Deliverance

In the Soul Care eCourse, watch lessons 32-39

Summary of Soul Care Principle #7: Deliverance

I grew up in a Bible-believing church, but I never heard anyone talk about casting out demons—with two exceptions. First, it would be mentioned if someone preached on a passage in the gospels in which Jesus cast out a demon. Second, on a rare occasion a missionary would visit our church and tell a story about someone who needed deliverance. But these were people from exotic places like Africa or Thailand; they weren't ever stories from people in the Western context. So I suppose the assumption I held in my youth was that demons only lived in Africa and Thailand and in other exotic places. Most of the time our worldview is not carefully thought through; there are many assumptions that arise from our experiences or lack of experiences.

When I was in seminary, however, I met a young man who was clearly demonized. He heard voices that were telling him to kill people; he would growl and snarl while you talked with him. I sat in on a deliverance session with him, led by one of my professors, Dr. John Ellenberger, who had experience in such things, but we couldn't get any demons out. The man had sin and was not willing to repent. That was my first exposure to deliverance ministry.

Many of us in the Western world do not have any experience or worldview for deliverance, but Jesus did. Deliverance ministry was normal for Jesus and the disciples. There are some problems that are physical, and they require a doctor's care or divine healing; there are other problems that are emotional, and they need Soul Care, inner healing, or counseling. And there are other problems that are spiritual, and the only solution is deliverance. You cannot cast out human, and you cannot educate, medicate, or counsel a demon. When the root of a problem is demonic, the only solution is deliverance. Jesus did deliverance ministry because He knew demons were real, and it was the only way to get certain people free. Sometimes I read a modern Bible commentator who writes that, in the first century, they didn't really understand psychological problems, and there weren't really demons. The people, according to the expert, just didn't understand. But Jesus wasn't a country bumpkin who couldn't discern the difference between a psychological problem and a demonic issue. He did deliverance because demons are real, and deliverance is necessary to get people free. We have to start with that assumption if we are to take Jesus seriously.

You cannot cast out human, and you cannot educate, medicate, or counsel a demon.

We are undergoing a significant change in worldview in the West. I grew up in a modern worldview watching cartoons like Scooby Doo. There was always a ghost, but by the end of the cartoon the ghost was unmasked, and we discovered that the ghost wasn't really a ghost; rather, it was a bad guy dressed up like a ghost. They were teaching us a worldview: "Behind every apparent supernatural phenomenon is a natural explanation. The supernatural world does not really interact with the natural world" (*Soul Care,* 2016, p. 206). But that is not the worldview of Jesus. Somewhere in the mid-1990s, however, I was watching a Scooby Doo cartoon and, as always, there was a ghost. But this time, at the end of the cartoon, the ghost was actually a ghost. They were teaching a new generation of children that behind an apparent supernatural phenomenon was an actual supernatural being you could interact with. This is the new world we live in and, as a result, far more people are experimenting with a variety of supernatural practices. Sadly, while the world around us has shifted its worldview, too often the church has been slow to change.

Spirits are part of the biblical worldview. The Old Testament deities like Baal, Moloch, Chemosh, Dagon, and others were demonic entities. There was no deliverance ministry done in the Old Testament. In history, deliverance ministry begins in the intertestamental period (between the Old and New Testaments). There are Jewish exorcists who begin to do deliverance ministry before Jesus came on the scene (which Jesus testifies to in Luke 11). A demon is also called an evil spirit, or an unclean spirit, or an impure spirit. They are fallen angelic beings that have rebelled against God and seek to indwell people to do them harm.

Can Christians Have Demons?

The big question people debate is: "Can Christians have demons?" I believe the answer is yes, but let's clear up our terminology to begin. Most of our English translations translate the Greek word, demonization, as "demon possession." But I think that is a poor translation of the Greek. The word possession implies ownership. I would argue that neither a believer, nor a non-believer, can be owned or possessed by a demon. God is the creator. He has ownership rights. Remember the story where someone challenges Jesus about paying taxes, and Jesus gets a coin and asks: "Whose image is this? And whose inscription?" They tell him it is Caesar's. "Then he said to them, 'Give back to Caesar what is Caesar's, and to God what is God's'" (Matthew 22:21). Just as the coin is stamped with the image of Caesar, so all humans are stamped with the image of God. We belong to God. Possession is not at stake. The Greek word simply means that a demon is indwelling, and it needs to be cast out. Imagine I handed you my water bottle, and you poured your drink into it: who does the bottle belong to? It is still my bottle. When someone has an indwelling demonic spirit, possession (ownership) has not changed.

Let's think about how discipleship works. There are two big components to discipleship: access and appropriation. First, we need to give Jesus access to our lives. He shines light into our hearts, and we need to walk in the light with God and others. We need to admit our sin, humble ourselves before God, and give Him access. When we give access to God, we gain access to the resources of Christ. We have everything we need in the heavenly realms to live a godly life (Ephesians chapter 1; 2 Peter 1).

But just because we now have all these heavenly resources doesn't mean we automatically live in victory. There is a second part of discipleship: we must learn how to appropriate the victories of Jesus into our life so we can overcome. When you came to faith in Christ, that act, important as it is, didn't eliminate all your struggles with sin. You have everything you need to live a godly life, but you still struggle with sin, and so do I. That is because we have to give Him access and appropriate his victories. When you came to faith in Christ, you didn't automatically eliminate and overcome all your wounds, hurts, and heartaches. You have to walk out your salvation; you have what you need to live a victorious life in Christ, but you have to give access and appropriate victories for healing and wholeness. Why, then, do we assume that when we came to faith in Christ the demons automatically left? That isn't how God deals with other areas of sanctification. We have to give access and appropriate the victories of Jesus.

Let me provide some reasons why I believe Christians can be demonized. (I never use the word possessed, because I believe it is a bad translation.) First, *Jesus always does his deliverance ministry with people of faith, with God-fearing people.* In the Gospels, there were no Christians yet, so people were either Jews or Gentiles. The vast majority of people Jesus does deliverance with are Jewish people; they are covenant people, people of faith. There are two exceptions: first, the Syrophoenician woman's daughter, and Jesus tells the woman that she has great faith. The second Gentile that Jesus does deliverance with is the man in Mark 5, the demoniac who lived in the tombs. But this man runs to Jesus, a clear display of faith; he runs for help. And after his deliverance, he begs to go with Jesus. Both Gentiles that Jesus did deliverance with displayed faith, and that is what allows anyone to enter into covenant relationship with God (see Romans 4). Jesus never goes into pagan villages and does deliverance with pagans who display no faith.

Jesus never goes into pagan villages and does deliverance with pagans who display no faith.

Second, *the Apostle John tells us to "test the spirits"* (1 John 4:1). He says this to the church about the church. He isn't telling them to test the spirits in their pagan neighbors.

Third, *Paul also tells the church* (in Corinth, 1 Corinthians) *to test the spirits.* Paul is writing to them about spiritual gifts in a church service, and he says, "I want you to know that no one who is speaking by the Spirit of God says, 'Jesus be cursed,' and no one can say, 'Jesus is Lord,' except by the Holy Spirit" (1 Corinthians 12:3). He is focused on the gift of prophecy, speaking a word from the Spirit. Why would he tell them that no one speaking by the Spirit can say Jesus is cursed? The vast majority of people converted in Corinth, and Ephesus, and similar contexts, were pagans. They were pluralistic, syncretistic people who worshiped many deities; when they came to faith in Christ, they simply added Jesus to their plethora of deities. Upon conversion they didn't always immediately and completely leave these other deities behind. Look at Acts 19, the story of the church at Ephesus, as an example. These people had come to faith in Christ, but they didn't burn their magic scrolls and forsake their magic arts until after the incident with the seven sons of Sceva. Paul knew that often these syncretistic practitioners came to faith in Christ but hadn't given up their magic arts. Getting them to completely leave their magic behind and step into deliverance was part of discipleship.

Fourth, *if demons were cast out upon conversion, then Jesus and the disciples wouldn't have needed to do deliverance.* They just would have needed to lead people to faith in Christ.

Fifth, some people argue that light and darkness cannot dwell in the same place, so they ask, *"How can the Holy Spirit and a demonic spirit live in the same person?" This is a bit of Old Testament theology.* In the Old Testament, when the clean came into contact with the unclean, the clean became defiled. But in the New Testament, when the clean came in contact with the unclean, the unclean was cleansed. For example, in the Old Testament you couldn't touch a leper without being defiled, but in the New Testament, Jesus touches a leper (Matthew 8), and He says, "Be clean." And the leper is cleansed. Jesus said in Luke 11:13: "If you then, though you are evil, know how to give good gifts to your children, how much more will your Father in heaven give the Holy Spirit to those who ask him!" Jesus calls us evil, yet He says that the Father is willing to deposit his Holy Spirit within us. God's New Testament strategy for sanctification is to put the Holy Spirit directly in the middle of our hot, messy life so He can make us clean from the inside out. The Spirit of God is in no way intimidated by evil or evil spirits, so He lets us come as we are, meets us where we are, indwells us like we are, and cleans us up from the inside out as we give Him access and appropriate the victories of Jesus.

Sixth, *Jesus tells a parable that indicates we shouldn't do deliverance on non-believers.* He said, "When an evil spirit comes out of anyone, it goes through arid places seeking rest and does not find it. Then it says, 'I will return to the house I left.' When it arrives, it finds the house swept clean and put in order. Then it goes and takes seven other spirits more wicked than itself, and they go in and live there. And the final condition of that person is worse than the first" (Luke 11:24-26). Look at the context: this discourse began with Jesus casting out a spirit from a mute man who then could speak. But the leaders said it was by the power of Beelzebul that Jesus drove out demons. Jesus explains that He was able to drive out demons because He is stronger than the strong man (Satan). "When a strong man, fully armed, guards his own house, his possessions are safe. But when someone stronger attacks and overpowers him, he takes away the armor in which the man trusted and divides up his plunder" (Luke 11:21, 22). The strong man in the parable is Satan. The stronger man who overpowers him is Jesus. The house is the person who is demonized, and the possessions are the demons. Jesus is saying the reason He can cast out demons with a spoken word is because He is stronger than Satan. But in the parable He tells at the end, Jesus is saying that if He does not live in the house (in the person), then the house is not protected. The enemy can come back, double down, and reinfest the person, making their final condition worse than at first. Deliverance ministry is part of discipleship, and only when someone has come to faith in Christ, and has Christ in them, are they safe from reinfestation.

Seventh, *in church history there have been many who testified to deliverance ministry being done in the church on believers as part of discipleship.* Hippolytus, for example, wrote a book called "The Apostolic Tradition" around A.D. 200. He said the church in his region did deliverance (exorcism) as part of its baptism rites. When converts came to Christ out of pagan backgrounds, they led them through teaching on monotheism (so they would leave behind all other deity worship), helped them learn how to walk in the power of the Holy Spirit for holiness, and then did their deliverance before they baptized people. They did deliverance on believers as part of discipleship.

Finally, *everyone I know who does deliverance ministry does deliverance on believers as part of discipleship.* The only people I know who argue against it don't do deliverance at all. Yet Jesus commanded the disciples to cast out demons in Matthew 10, and then in Matthew 28 he commanded them to "Go and make disciples of all nations, baptizing them in the name of the Father and of the Son and of the Holy Spirit, and teaching them to obey everything I have commanded you" (Matthew 28:19, 20). I believe deliverance is part of the Great Commission; Jesus commanded the apostles to teach us to obey everything He had commanded them—and He had commanded them to cast out demons.

How Do Spirits Enter?

How do spirits enter a person? The big answer is sin. We don't need live in fear. If we are walking humbly with God, confessing our sin as we commit it, and not living in a state of rebellion, we will be fine. God has more grace than we have sin. But if we live a lifestyle of rebellion, that can be an open door for the enemy. Samuel said to King Saul that rebellion is like witchcraft! There are certain types of sins that are more likely to lead to demonization. This is not an all-inclusive list, but let me provide a few examples.

God has more grace than we have sin.

Witchcraft, occult activity, and other religious practices lead to demonization. If you worship other deities, you are going to get demonic spirits. You are giving the enemy access by entering into relationship with those deities. Sometimes it was not you who engaged in those things, but, perhaps, your mother practiced witchcraft or ancestor worship, and the spirits are passed on to you.

Sexual sin can also be an entry point for demonic spirits. Demons can be transferred through sex. Let me give you some examples: prostitution leads to demonization every time; I have never seen an exception. When someone exchanges sex for drugs, money, power, position, or anything else, they will be demonized and need deliverance. God calls us to a monogamous marital relationship: one man, one woman, in a marriage covenant for life. When we step outside the boundaries of that marriage covenant, there is a chance of demonization. It isn't a certainty, but we are no longer protected by the covenant of marriage. Monogamy isn't just safe sex; it is safe spirituality. If we have fifty sexual partners in our lifetime, there is a far greater chance of picking up transferred demonic spirits. If we live in serial adultery, or if that activity has been a part of our family history, there is a much greater change of demonization—because now you have sexual immorality and rebellion combined.

Addiction can lead to demonization. Again, it isn't only our addictive behaviors. Demonization can also be inherited through a parent and/or grandparent who has struggled with addiction.

Sadly, physical, emotional, and sexual abuse can also result in demonization. In my experience, when there is penetration in sexual abuse, it always results in demonization. When there is fondling without penetration, it is still probable, though not definite.

Symptoms

What are the symptoms of demonization? How do we know if we have demons? The most common symptom is anxiety. Not all anxiety is the result of demonization; people can have anxiety because of identity issues, fear, wounds, and all kinds of other things. But when a demon is present, anxiety is very common.

Often people with demons hear voices, or they have thoughts that are intrusive. They have thoughts that are not their own, and they can't seem to shut them off. They can live in victory over these thoughts and temptations; demons cannot force a person to do anything. But the thoughts are like a dripping faucet and, even though they submit themselves to God, the thoughts keep coming. The thoughts can be sexual in nature, condemning thoughts, blasphemous thoughts, suicidal thoughts, or a variety of dark things. The person prays about it and claims appropriate Scriptural promises, but they just can't get the leaky faucet to stop dripping. After deliverance, the intrusions stop, because they weren't the person's thoughts—they were those of a demonic presence that needed to be cast out.

Some people with demonic spirits struggle with anger and rage. It is a demonically inspired anger. In Mark 5 the demoniac wrestles with this, and it leads him to acts of violence and even supernatural strength to break his chains.

People with indwelling demons often feel tormented or tortured. This is a very common thing that people say when they are demonized. After deliverance, they feel relief from the inner torment.

Let me end by talking about the most common symptoms for people who have sexual abuse spirits. Not all people who have these symptoms have been sexually abused themselves; it is possible that one of their parents or grandparents was sexually abused, and the person inherited these spirits and the symptoms. If you have sexual abuse spirits, you may experience some of these symptoms.

First, *people who inherit sexual abuse spirits* (you cannot inherit them from your siblings, cousins, or aunts/uncles; they must come through your parents/grandparents) *often have erotic sexual thoughts long before puberty.* It isn't developmentally possible for a five-year-old to lust; that is most often demonic. Second, *many people with sexual abuse spirits will have sexual thoughts/images during sacred spaces*—like worship, Bible reading, and prayer. Third, *people with sexual abuse spirits often feel a dark presence in their room at night, especially their bedroom.* It feels like a bullying, intimidating presence. Fourth, *they often experience sleep paralysis; they feel pinned to the bed, and they want to cry out Jesus' name, but can't.* This typically only lasts a short period of time. Fifth, *sometimes these dark spirits will give perverted dreams.* The types of sexual dreams indicate the kind of abuse that you or those above you have suffered in the family. If you are having dreams, for example, where children are being touched, it is because someone was touched as a child (you, or one of your parents, or grandparents). Sixth, *sometimes the demon will engage the person in sexual activity.* A person will wake up in the night and feel like someone is performing a sex act on them, but no one is there doing so. If the partner is male, that is the Incubus. If it is a female partner, that is the Succubus. Seventh, *occasionally the spirit will scratch or bruise the person.* And finally, *it is not uncommon for people with sexual abuse spirits to find it hard to sleep through the night;* they often have disrupted sleep cycles until they are delivered. (Clearly, not everyone who has sleep problems has demons!)

How Do We Get Free?

How do we get free from demonic spirits? Before casting out demons, the most important preparation work is breaking ground. Ground is a legal right for a demonic spirit to stay. It is an access point. There are three major access points. First, *we must make sure our sins are confessed;* unconfessed or unrepented-of sin is an access point. If a person is not willing to repent of a sin, the demon can remain. God won't trump your will; I can't trump your will. Second, *demons can hide in secrets.* The most common secret is a family secret. For example, more than a half dozen times now I have been doing deliverance and I knew from the Holy Spirit that the person was conceived in rape. In each of those cases, I had the person go back and check with their mother, and it was confirmed. There are only two ways to uncover secrets: natural knowledge or supernatural knowledge. We need to talk to our families, or we need to hear it from God if our families will not talk to us. Third, *demons can have ground because of curses.*

There are three types of curses: (1) Religious curses. For example, someone may have been dedicated as a baby through Santeria or some other form of witchcraft. A dedication done in any name but Jesus' name is a curse. The parents want to bless, but demons never bless, they only curse. (2) Behavioral curses. When a family continues to sin in the same way generation after generation, it becomes a curse, a demonically reinforced pattern of behavior. We often have to break the curse to cast the demon out and have it stay out. (3) Word curses. Sometimes these are the things that are spoken over us in a house where there is emotional abuse. Statements like "you'll never amount to anything" or "I wish you were never born." The curse must be broken for the demon to be cast out and stay out. Sometimes these are the things we say over ourselves, like, "I will never trust anyone again." We are making an agreement with the enemy, and that curse must be broken before we can be free.

The ground should be broken prior to deliverance. I always have people go through *Soul Care* and do the work before I meet with anyone for deliverance. I have included a methodology in the *Soul Care* book, and in the eCourse, but the most complete training I offer is through our Deliverance Training Workship. I do two livestreams every year to equip people in deliverance. You can find out more information about those on our website, www.renewalinternational.org .

Experiences

(1) "There is a supernatural sphere with supernatural beings, and they do interact with our world" (*Soul Care,* 2016, p. 207). What experiences do you have interacting with the supernatural world around us? Jesus did deliverance ministry. Deliverance was a normal part of Jesus' kingdom ministry. Does your worldview align with Jesus' worldview? What experiences have you had concerning deliverance ministry?

(2) One of the enemy's strategies is to make us afraid. But fear is a tool of the enemy to keep us from freedom and fullness in Christ. Jesus isn't afraid, and you are in Christ. The church at Ephesus was afraid when they stopped worshiping demonic spirits like Artemis; they were afraid of being attacked. Paul spends the first three chapters of Ephesians helping believers understand they are in Christ and Christ is in them, that they do not need to be afraid because Jesus is the unchallenged King of the universe. Meditate on Ephesians 1-3 with this in mind. And remember, these believers repented of their demonic worship after they had converted (read through Acts 19). Do you have any fear about the spiritual world that needs to be overcome?

(3) Take time to do a family inventory. Have there been any other religious practices by you, your parents, grandparents? Occult activity, witchcraft, secret societies (Masons, Eastern Star, etc.), Santeria, ancestor worship, and the like? Have you or your parents/grandparents experienced any abuse—physical, emotional, or sexual? Was there sexual immorality in your family tree? Adultery, promiscuity, sexual perversions? Is there a pattern of anger, bitterness, resentment, grudge-holding, or rage in your family? Murder, abortion, bloodshed? Any history of mental illness, depression, anxiety, panic attacks, or the like? (I believe people can suffer mental illness; parts of our brain may not be operating properly, just as other parts of our body can fail us. But I also know that sometimes demons can manifest in these ways, and counselors without a spiritual worldview can diagnose the symptoms and miss the demonic roots.) Any suicides or suicide attempts? Is addiction an issue for you or those in your family tree? Do people in your family struggle with fear, shame, control, ma-

nipulation? The more we discover these patterns, the more prevalent they are, and the more likely there will be need for deliverance. If you have any combination of these symptoms, keep your eyes on Jesus; He isn't nervous. Go back to identity work, make sure you work through Soul Care, and then seek deliverance, if needed.

(4) Take an inventory of symptoms. Are you struggling with any of the symptoms we have spoken of? Anxiety, suicide ideations/thoughts, rage/anger, voices/intrusive thoughts, blasphemous thoughts? Sexual abuse symptoms (early erotic sexual thoughts, sexual thoughts in sacred spaces, a dark presence in your room at night, perverse sexual dreams, sexual visitations in the night, etc.)? Which ones have plagued you? Have they been a problem for anyone else in the family?

(5) Everyone engages in spiritual warfare. Jesus was tempted yet lived without sin. Discipleship involves giving Jesus access and appropriating Jesus' victories. Are there any areas where you are not giving Jesus access? Are there areas where Jesus has shined light into your soul but you have not been willing to own what He is illuminating? Any areas where you have not been willing to repent? We have to break the ground by giving Jesus access. We also need to learn how to appropriate the victories of Jesus so we can live free. Where have you been honest and confessional but not yet found victory in your life? What potential keys to the Kingdom do you need to gain victory over? Have you engaged in humbly walking in the light with others? Prayer and fasting for victory? Seeking God to deal with the root issues and not just manage sin and fight symptoms? Is deliverance one of the tools you need to appropriate victory?

(6) Read Mark 5:1-20. Meditate on this passage. What does the Lord show you? Why was deliverance normal for Jesus but is not normal for many of us today? If Jesus is the same yesterday, today, and forever, shouldn't Jesus be doing these things in the church today? Where has your Western worldview messed up your biblical understanding?

(7) Be sure to break the access points. Make sure you have brought all your sin into the light with God and that your confessions are current. Have the conversations that you can with your family to make sure you have uncovered any secrets you can. And break the curses that are there. Galatians 3 tells us that Jesus died on a cross to become a curse for us, to break the curse of sin and Satan over us. Claim Jesus' victories on the cross and break the curses in Jesus' name. There is more information on curses in our Deliverance Training Workship. Take time to review the work on your family sin patterns and break off behavioral curses (repetitive generational sins). Break off the word curses. (You may refer to your work on wounds to help you remember.) Break off the religious curses. All religions are ceremonial and covenantal in nature, but a ceremony (like a dedication) done in any other deity's name is a curse. Demons never bless, even if the people holding the ceremony mean it for good. The major ceremonies include: dedication, initiation, healing, power, protection, prosperity, fertility (for land or human reproduction).

(8) If you feel you need deliverance, see if your church has a deliverance ministry, or you may want to come to a Soul Care Conference. You can find where Soul Care Conferences are being held on our website, www.renewalinternational.org, under events. Come with the small group that you have been processing this workbook with.

(9) Is there a deliverance ministry in your church? If so, you may want to go for ministry, or you may want to join the ministry and help others get free. Not all methodologies are equal. The test of a good methodology is that it gets people free and they stay free, and that the model is reproducible and can be used to equip others to be effective in deliverance ministries. You may want to attend our Deliverance Training Workshop, learn more about deliverance, and better equip yourself in the methodology I use. It has been used on every continent on the planet, and hundreds of thousands of people have found freedom in Christ. If there is not a deliverance ministry in your church, you may want to start one. Do not, however, start a deliverance ministry without the support and blessing of your leadership. Do not be divisive. Is the Lord leading you to get involved?

(10) Jesus gave his disciples authority to cast out demons. Authority is both positional and developmental. Spiritual authority is rooted in identity, expanded in intimacy, and activated by faith. We have to develop our authority. If you want to get involved in deliverance ministry or want to see more of the Kingdom of God expand in and around you, you must grow in spiritual authority. I encourage you to read my book *Spiritual Authority.* Read it and work out the practices in your life.

Notes

Notes

CONCLUSION

Soul Care is not a book to be read like a novel, nor a conference to be attended in three days, and neither is it an eCourse to sit through and watch. Soul Care is a lifestyle to be adopted and integrated into your daily existence. You have to live it out, and that takes time.

Often people come to me for help, and I ask them, "Have you worked through the book?" They respond, "I read it." I push a little harder. "Yes, but did you do the work?" They reluctantly admit that they did not really do the work. In the Western world we have wrongly assumed that if we knew the right things, we would do the right things. We have substituted knowledge for integration and learning for obedience. Life change doesn't occur because we know these truths; life change occurs because we integrate the truths and live them out.

Let me leave you with a few final things to keep in mind.

Persevere Through the Process

Integrating the principles of Soul Care is a process, not an event. "It takes one day longer than a lifetime to finally get well. When you meet Jesus face to face, you will be like Him; in the meantime, you are on a journey" (*Soul Care*, 2016, p. 241). Therefore, we need to press in and press through, and for that to take place, we need to process deeply. Too often people have the wrong goal in their hearts: their chief goal is to feel better. So they press in only long enough to alleviate the pain, but they don't press in and press through to the freedom and fullness that is their inheritance in Christ. Don't settle short of your redemptive potential; press in and press through.

Walk in the Light

We have to keep walking in the light with God and others. This is vital to remaining humble before the Lord. "God is close to the brokenhearted. God is irresistibly attracted to the contrite of heart. God draws near to the humble, but the proud walk alone. Don't be too proud to get help"

(*Soul Care,* 2016, p. 243). The enemy is the prince of darkness, but God is light. Don't let the enemy persuade you to live in the dark; there is no freedom there.

Prioritize Your Time with God

In my early twenties I decided to make my time with God a non-negotiable commitment, and I have never allowed anything to get in the way of that decision. It has been one of the most important decisions I have ever made. There is healing in God's presence, and we must spend time with Him to access his healing power. In the beginning, when Jen and I had our marriage crisis, I did not know how authentic life change worked. I just kept coming to Jesus and asking Him what to do, and whatever He showed me, I simply said yes. Meet with God, learn how to hear Him through the Scriptures and through the Spirit, and do what He tells you to do. The secret to success is to find what God wants and do it, no matter what the personal cost.

Go for the Roots

Too often churches focus on behavior management and sin management, but leaders and members don't get to the heart and soul issues. We must go for the roots; we have to fight the disease and not focus on the symptoms. Jesus told us that it is out of the overflow of the heart that our sin and dysfunction arise. So, one of my favorite Soul Care questions is, "What's underneath that?" Why do I do what I do, think what I think, and feel what I feel? God knows our hearts, and He knows how to address the issues of the heart.

Be Patient

Life change is hard, and we must be patient with ourselves (and others) and learn to persevere in active waiting on God. Psalm 37:7 says, "Be still before the Lord and wait patiently for him." This is an active waiting; it is learning to trust God and do the work of the heart and soul with Him.

Waiting is hard, painful, difficult soul work. "The root word for wait here is to dance, whirl, writhe. There is a tension. You wait for God to deliver you. But you wait for God's answers in a whirling dance of emotions, disappointments, doubts, and agony, writhing in prayer and coming to a place of surrender, trust, and obedience. Resolve to keep coming, keep trusting, keep surrendering, and keep obeying" (*Soul Care,* 2016, p. 245).

So, wherever you are on the journey, whether you feel stuck and hopeless or feel like you are walking in significant levels of freedom and fullness, there is always more. There is always more freedom that we can experience in Christ; there is always more of his presence and power to know, encounter, and participate in. There is always a new level of depth, a fresh encounter, a deeper experience of love, joy, and peace. Press in, and press through into more freedom, fullness, and intimacy in Christ!

Experiences

(1) What is God calling you to do to keep growing deeper in Christ? Take time to sit with the Lord and ask Him about it; wait upon the Lord for wisdom and revelation. What are your next steps and stages of development? Where do you need to press in to God for more?

(2) Have you established a non-negotiable time with God in your life? Is there anything in your time with God that you need to adjust to refresh it? Is your current spiritual rhythm working? Are you connecting deeply with God? Are you loving God and people more this year than you did two years ago? Are you experiencing more freedom and fullness than you were? If it isn't working, then you have to change things. Ask the Lord for insight. What should you do differently? (You can read the chapter on intimacy with God in *The Soul Care Leader* for more insight on this.).

(3) Is there any area of these seven principles in Soul Care that God is calling you to do more work on, to go deeper? What area? What do you need to do to take things deeper? Is there some Scripture you need to study and meditate on? Is there some other spiritual discipline you need to engage in? Other books you need to work through to get to the next level? Other honest conversations with people that you need to have?

(4) Is there anything God has been asking you to do as you worked through this workbook that you haven't followed through with? Don't resist the Holy Spirit. Go back and do what God has asked you to do. Is there a particular area where you haven't done the work? You read it, but you didn't do the work? Go back and do the work.

(5) Is there anyone God wants you to pass Soul Care on to? Is God calling you to work through Soul Care with another person or to start a Soul Care group?

(6) Is there an area where God is calling you to press in and press through? Can you see any place where your goal was just to feel better rather than experience all the freedom and fullness Jesus has for you? What do you need to do to press in and press through? What does that look like in this situation for you?

(7) Are there any areas where you have been battling with symptoms but you have not yet gotten to the root? You may want to read the chapters titled Getting to the Roots, and Talking vs. Processing, in my book, *The Soul Care Leader,* to help you get to the root issues.

Notes

Notes

164

ABOUT THE AUTHOR

Dr. Rob Reimer's passion is to see the Kingdom of God advance through spiritual renewal. Rob began Renewal International to assist pastors, leaders, and churches globally to equip the people of God to live in freedom in Christ, and to walk in the fullness and power of the Holy Spirit.

Passionate about Jesus, personally transparent, and saturated in the Word, his books, including *Soul Care, River Dwellers, Spiritual Authority, Deep Faith, Pathways to the King, The Soul Care Leader, Calm in the Storm* and *The Tenderness of Jesus* incorporate lessons God taught him over the years through life, marriage, and ministry. During conferences, Rob not only teaches these lessons, but provides activities for participants to begin working them into their lives. These transformative experiences challenge people to walk in the light with God and others and help people practice hearing from God and accessing His power for ministry. Without Jesus, we have nothing to offer!

In addition to his work with Renewal International, Dr. Reimer has served as Professor of Pastoral Theology at Alliance University in NY, NY, and as the founding and lead pastor of a church in New England.

Explore more of Rob's resources,
view his itinerary, or invite him to speak at
www.renewalinternational.org

ALSO BY DR. ROB REIMER

River Dwellers
Living in the Fullness of the Spirit

Did you ever wish there was more to your Christian life? Too often the Christian life is reduced to going to church, attending meetings, serving God, and doing devotions. But Jesus promised us abundant life—a deep, intimate, satisfying connection with the living God. How do we access the abundant life that Jesus promised? The key is the presence and life of the Holy Spirit within us.

Jesus said that the Spirit of God flows within us like a river—He is the River of Life. But we need to dwell in the river in order to access the Spirit's fullness.

In *River Dwellers,* Dr. Rob Reimer offers a deep look at life in the Spirit and provides practical strategies for dwelling in the River of Life. We will explore the fullness of the Spirit, tuning into the promptings of the Spirit, walking in step with the Spirit, and developing sensitivity to the presence of God in our lives. This resource will guide you toward becoming a full-time river dweller, even in the midst of life's most difficult seasons when the river seems to run low.

Together let's become River Dwellers, living where the fullness of God flows so that we can carry living water to a world dying of thirst!

Pathways to the King

Living a Life of Spiritual Renewal and Power

We need revival. The church in America desperately needs revival. There are pockets of it happening right now, but we need another Great Awakening. About forty years ago, the church was impacted by the church growth movement. The goal of the movement was to get the church focused on the Great Commission—taking the Good News about Jesus to the entire world. The church was off mission, and the movement was a necessary course correction. But it didn't work. Many people came to Christ as a result of this outreach emphasis, and I am grateful for that. More churches are now focused on evangelism, helping people come to know Jesus, than they were before the movement. But we have fewer people attending church now (percentage-wise) than ever before in the history of the United States. We need revival.

This book is about how we can usher in revival and also about the price that we must pay to experience it. I believe we have a part to play in seeing the next great spiritual awakening. God wants us to be carriers of His Kingdom. He wants us to experience the reality and fullness of His Kingdom, and he wants us to expand the Kingdom to others—just like Jesus did. In order to do that, I believe we must follow eight Kingdom Pathways of Spiritual Renewal: Personalizing our Identity in Christ, Pursuing God, Purifying Ourselves, Praising, Praying Kingdom Prayers, Claiming Promises, Passing the Tests, and Persisting. These eight pathways are discussed in great detail, are securely rooted in biblical truths, and are illustrated by compelling examples from Scripture and from my life, the lives of believers in my community, and in the lives of great Christians throughout history.

Available at www.DrRobReimer.com

Deep Faith

Developing Faith that Releases the Power of God

Jesus said, "Very truly I tell you, all who have faith in me will do the works that I have been doing, and they will do even greater things than these" (John 14:12). The extraordinary promise of Jesus is that we can do Kingdom works that He did—cast out demons, heal the sick, save the lost, and set the captives free.

Jesus wants to advance His Kingdom through us. But this promise comes with a condition: the level of our Kingdom activity is dependent upon our faith.

There are promises in Heaven that God wants to release, but they cannot be released without faith. There are miracles that God wants to do that cannot be done without faith. There are answers to prayer that God wants to unleash that cannot be unleashed without faith. There are works of the Kingdom that God wants to accomplish that cannot be accomplished unless the people of God develop deeper faith. But there is hope for all of us, because faith can be developed.

Faith opens doors and creates opportunities for accessing God's power against all odds. Faith is a difference maker, a future shaper, a bondage breaker, a Kingdom mover. In this moving book, Dr. Rob Reimer challenges readers to develop deep faith that can release the works of the Kingdom. Faith is not static; it is dynamic. We can and must take an intentional path toward developing our faith if we want to see the works of the Kingdom in greater measure.

Spiritual Authority

Partnering with God to Release the Kingdom

Jesus gave His disciples authority to preach the good news of the Kingdom of God and to cast out demons, heal the sick, save the lost, and set the captives free. Everywhere Jesus went, the Kingdom came with power. There was no proclamation of the gospel without a demonstration of power. It was the authentic demonstration of Jesus' power through His followers that ignited the greatest spiritual movements in the first century. Today, we are becoming more like the spiritual climate in the first century then like 1950s America. In a pluralistic, syncretistic society where all deities are considered equal, only the unequal display of Jesus' power will convince people of the supremacy of Christ. The key to demonstrating the power of the King is authority, and authority is not just positional; it is developmental. Spiritual authority is rooted in identity, expanded in intimacy, and activated by faith. This book takes an in-depth look at how we can grow in identity, intimacy, and faith so that we can develop our authority and release the Kingdom.

Also available in Spanish (Autoridad Espirituald).

Calm in the Storm

How God Can Redeem a Crisis to Advance His Kingdom

There is nothing like a crisis to reveal the cracks in the walls of our soul. But God promises to redeem all things that come into our lives to make us more like Jesus. We have experienced a unique crisis in our day and age, COVID-19. It has created fear, death, and will leave economic disaster in its wake. In this book, I don't just talk about how we can survive this crisis, or how we can access the peace of God in tumultuous times. I talk about how God can redeem a crisis in our personal lives to take us deeper into maturity and intimacy with Christ. And how this particular crisis could potentially lead to revival if the church processes it well. We stand on the precipice of an unprecedented opportunity to be purified and mobilized on mission to advance the Kingdom of God in our generation.

The Tenderness of Jesus

An Invitation to Experience the Savior

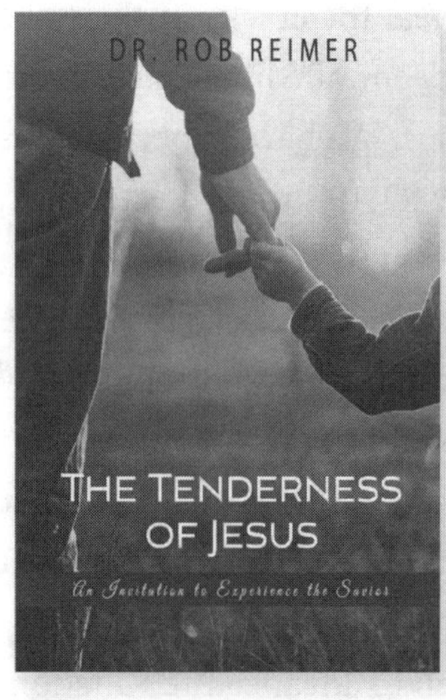

The world is a broken place marred by evil, and evil's influence impacts us all. It is often difficult for people to grasp what God is like in a world such as ours. Jesus shows us the heart of God in a world of heartache. He is the most beautiful, compelling, tender person who has lived.

Jesus is the radiance of God's glory. He shines forth what God is like; He is a beacon of light that cuts through the darkness of evil and radiates the goodness of God. He is the exact representation of God the Father. If you want to know what God is like, look to Jesus. Don't look through the lens of evil or the lenses of either the church or religion. Look to Jesus. That is why He came. The world is not an exact representation of God. The church is not an exact representation of God. Jesus is. He came to freshly present what the Father is like to those of us who are spiritually impaired by a world of suffering.

The Tenderness of Jesus, in many ways, is my most personal book to date. I invite you to listen in as I write to my four young adult children about the tenderness of Jesus Christ. Come sit with us around the dinner table. May this fresh glimpse of Jesus heal your broken heart and reignite your spiritual fervor.

Soul Care

7 Transformational Principles for a Healthy Soul

Soul Care explores seven principles that can lead to lasting transformation and freedom for all who struggle with a broken, damaged, and sin-stained soul.

Brokenness grasps for the soul of humanity. We are broken body, soul, and spirit, and we need the healing touch of Jesus. *Soul Care* explores seven principles that are profound healing tools of God: securing your identity, repentance, breaking family sin patterns, forgiving others, healing wounds, overcoming fears, and deliverance.

Dr. Rob Reimer challenges readers to engage in an interactive, roll-up-your-sleeves and get messy process—a journey of self-reflection, Holy Spirit inspiration, deep wrestling, and surrender. It is a process of discovering yourself in true community and discovering God as He pierces through the layers of your heart.

Life change is hard. But these principles, when packaged together and lived out, can lead to lasting transformation, freedom, and a healthy soul. *Soul Care* encourages you to gather a small group of comrades in arms, read and process together, open your souls to one another, access the presence and power of God together, and journey together into the freedom and fullness of Christ.

The Soul Care Leader

Healthy Living and Leading

How do we live a healthy life and lead others into spiritual, emotional and relational health and wholeness?

That is the focus of this book.

Trying to help others find freedom and wholeness is draining work. What do we do to become healthy and maintain our well-being? What are the practices and rhythms we need to engage in to be effective Soul Care practitioners? How do we create a culture where life-change flourishes? How do we minister in the power of the Spirit so we can lead others into breakthroughs?

Too often people are talking about the same problems that they were talking about several years ago, but they aren't finding a path to freedom. We need to help people get to the roots and not merely manage their dysfunction and sin. These are the questions and topics that this book will seek to equip you in as you seek to live and lead people into freedom and fullness in Christ.

Authentic

Cultivating Authentic Relationship With God

How do we develop a deep lasting intimacy with God? One of the problems with being a Christ follower is that we can substitute religious expressions and religious behaviors for authentic experiences and encounters without even know we are doing it. The longer we go to church the more we know the right words to say and the right things to do, but we can easily say those words and do those things without transformational intimacy with Jesus. We can start with significant, transformational encounters with God, and end up with dusty old religion. In *Authentic*, we will explore the following: What is religion and how do we avoid falling into its traps and snares? How does intimacy with God and people work? How do we develop depth with God and sustain it over a lifetime? What are the practices and attitudes that we can develop to help us draw near to God so we can learn to live an authentic spiritual life in Christ? We don't want to settle for the counterfeit, when Jesus offers us abundant life.